JOSEPH – a Fruitful Bough

JOSEPH
a Fruitful Bough

Robert McPheat

JOHN RITCHIE LTD
CHRISTIAN PUBLICATIONS

40 Beansburn, Kilmarnock, Scotland

ISBN 0 946351 84 8

Copyright © 1999 by John Ritchie Ltd.
40 Beansburn, Kilmarnock, Scotland

Typeset by John Ritchie Ltd., Kilmarnock
Printed by Bell & Bain Ltd., Glasgow

Contents

Preface

When asked by brother Malcolm Radcliffe if I knew whether Robert had written a book, I replied that I did not know. I added that I thought it most unlikely, as he always said he preferred to "preach rather than write". I enquired from Greta, Robert's wife, and to my surprise and delight discovered that he had, at the request of brother Denis Gilpin, commenced to write on the life of Joseph, and as far as she knew had completed the task. Having made further enquiry with the help of brother Eddie Taylor, the original manuscript was located and when I began to read it my first reaction was that this was indeed a treasure that would be appreciated by many saints who knew and loved our dear brother.

Those who listened to Robert preach will detect in this book the same style of not only interpretation but also practical application of the Scriptures. He always showed a keen interest in young believers and I have cause to thank God for the way he influenced and encouraged me as a young believer. The young reader will find that here there is a wealth of spiritual guidance available for them from his pen.

In his ministry he loved to exalt the person of our Lord Jesus and readers will discover in these pages that this theme is predominant as he uses Joseph as a type of Christ. Ministry should be given with a view to lifting the saints on to higher ground, and we are confident that within this volume whether it be exhortative, devotional or Christ-exalting, there will be "bread enough and to spare" (Luke 15:17) to satisfy the need of every believer. This we are sure would be on the heart of the writer as he penned these pages less than three years before the Lord called him home.

We readily commend this book to all as a fitting tribute to a devoted and faithful servant of Christ. I would like to record our gratitude to all who have helped to make this book available to the saints; those already mentioned, also my daughter Eunice for the typing of the manuscript, and brother Bert Cargill for his valuable help in the editing, layout and proof reading.

Robert Miller
Gorebridge
May 1999

About the Author

Robert McLean McPheat was born at Airdrie in Scotland on 13th November 1933, the third child in a family of six. In 1947 a Mr Wilding had gospel meetings in the nearby village of Greengairs and a school friend of Robert's, John Clelland, attended and was saved. He then spoke to Robert at school about his salvation and having expressed an interest in these matters they both went into the school gym where Robert accepted the Lord Jesus as his Saviour as a young lad of fourteen. He subsequently was baptised in the Hebron Hall at Airdrie and received into fellowship in the assembly at Plains. He often spoke of the help he was given by the saints during his time in fellowship there, and in particular by brother John King, of whom he spoke lovingly as his spiritual father.

In 1951 he came to Newtongrange in Midlothian to work at the Lady Victoria Colliery, travelling home each weekend. He married Margaret (Greta) Robertson in January 1953 and they were received into fellowship in Newtongrange assembly two months later, setting up home in Mayfield, a nearby village where the assembly is now located. From the beginning of their marriage their home was constantly open to the saints, and we have many happy memories of fellowship enjoyed there. He served faithfully as an overseer in the assembly and his guidance and care were greatly valued at a time when the testimony was faced with many difficult problems.

It was evident in those early years that the Lord had gifted Robert in preaching the gospel and teaching the Word of God, and in October 1967 he was heartily commended to the work of the Lord by the assemblies at Plains and

Newtongrange. His first meetings after commendation were in Northern Ireland where he was warmly received and where he often made many visits. His first meetings at his home assembly were in 1968 in a tent pitched on the site of our present Gospel Hall in Mayfield. His sphere of service took him throughout the UK, to Canada and the USA, and also to the island of Jersey where on 25th July 1990 the Lord called him home.

Foreword

Joseph, of the book of Genesis, has left us an example that we may follow. He towers above the other sons of the patriarch Jacob. He seems nearer of kin to the New Testament Christian than any other individual so far met within that book - I speak in relation to pleasing his father, and to such other aspects of his life which we will again consider in these pages.

- His obedience, his submission, his behaviour under excessive envy, his resilience to adapt to whatever sphere God's providence and sovereign guidance placed him in, and his outstanding purity and decided convictions not to be the minion of his seductress, have been every youth's example.

- Then in the sore temptation in the prison when the iron entered into his soul, when the word of the Lord tried him, when the dreams of his youth were darkened by the gloom of the dungeon, his hands were so willingly stretched out to serve - in the midst of his own grief to notice the sadness of others.

- In his rise to greatness because of the dream of Pharaoh and the jolting of a man's memory, we admire his disposition before the greatest monarch on earth, his calm confidence in God and the conviction that God would answer the emergency of circumstances.

- His experiences of being loved, envied, stripped, sold, tempted and falsely accused, were deep afflictions which broke the man but preserved him. In the moment of crisis he showed a diligence and a sensitivity begotten only in the man with whom God has taken dealings.

As this is not the first book on Joseph, neither will it be the last: no man, or group of men, has the monopoly of divine truth. It is nevertheless our prayer that this attempt to put together what has been preached upon during these last thirty years will be a blessing to many.

Robert McPheat
Gorebridge
September 1987

CHAPTER 1

Introduction:
Joseph as a Type of Christ

It would be informative to put on record some of the obvious instances where the features of Christ come out in Joseph. Even as we do this, it is wise to understand that all typology comes short of reality. While the shadow is of the body, it is as nothing to the substance. Luther said, "Why sit beside a candle (law) when the sun is risen (Christ)?"

Joseph's long looked for birth was like our Saviour's
Blessing generally comes in its appointed season. Joseph's evidence of early piety is so akin to that of the blessed Lord Jesus: His visit to the temple, among the learned asking and answering questions. His slowness to leave the sacred courts was an offence to His mother, but His reply was profound: "Wist ye not that I must be about My Father's business?" (Luke 2:49). Joseph is the well-loved son of his father. Christ is described as "My Son" (Psalm 2:7), "My beloved Son" (Matt 3:17), "the only begotten Son" (John 1:18). Prophetic language speaks of Him as "My darling from the power of the dog" (Psalm 22:20).

Joseph's coat was like Christ's Anointing
The Father could no longer suppress His pleasure in such a Son. The coat had many colours, but it would have one more - it would have blood upon it. God must rend the heavens, the symbolic dove will tell of the peace as well as the pleasure Christ gave the Father. The voice is heard in the

13

ears of sinful man and of the choicest of men, John the Baptist; but to Christ alone was the voice addressed "My beloved Son" (Matt 3:17). God thrills at every thought, mention, and act of Christ. The coat is Israel's response to Joseph's character: "A wise son maketh a glad father" (Prov 15:20); "A son honoureth his father" (Mal 1:6).

Joseph was the best of brothers

Nowhere will you find an accusation levelled at him for foolishness, lack of diligence, or laziness. Nowhere will you find recorded either at Nazareth or Capernaum that any flaw existed in Christ's character, His disposition, His craftsmanship and the prices He charged as a carpenter. Isaiah says, "who is blind but My servant, or deaf as My messenger that I sent" (Isaiah 42:19). To all the things that attracted others He was blind, to all the sounds that attracted others He was deaf. If it is to be shown the kingdoms of the world, He is blind; if it is a suggestion from the lips of Peter to avoid the cross, He is deaf. No family ever had a brother in it like Joseph. His piety was a rebuke to their iniquity. When the Lord was here there was excessive proof of the presence of evil powers, even in the synagogue.

Joseph grieved for his father's testimony

He told his father of his brothers' evil behaviour. When Christ came into the temple He saw so much that was removed from His Father's mind in that place which should have been approached with joy. Thieves and robbers were installed, merchandise had taken the place of sacrifice, and moneychangers' percentage was more in vogue than piety.

Joseph's revelations were rejected

What he had to declare of his dreams was from God, was unalterable, and was for their well-being. The revelations were to bring them God's mind. As with the dress, so with his dreams, they could not abide the consequence of his disclosures. The daily attacks upon him came from all quarters.

Joseph was directly sent by his father

No type in Scripture comes over so forcefully as this. "The Father sent the Son to be the Saviour of the world" (1 John 4:14). He said, "I came forth from the Father (pre-existence), and am come into the world (incarnation): again I leave the world (crucifixion), and go to the Father (ascension)" (John 16:28). The most endearing features of His lovely life were those aspects of it which brought pleasure and glory to His Father, even in His speech. He would not claim originality, but "I do nothing of Myself; but as My Father hath taught Me, I speak these things" (John 8:28). While those instances of fellowship between divine Persons may be difficult for us to understand - prayers, sighs, groans, tears and strong cryings - they are beautiful to behold, and are the basis of the longings of unfulfilled lives.

Joseph did his father's will

This has now brought him only hours away from his most painful experiences. How hollow are the voices that always link the will of God to success, acceptance, popularity, and running with the tide. Biblical records prove, and the life of Christ authenticates, that the pathway of the Man of the Father's pleasure is strewn with persecutions and opposition, with the wind constantly in His face. As God's stone He will be rejected, as the Prophet in His own country they will endeavour to thrust Him over the brow of the hill upon which their city is built.

Joseph was slandered

"Behold this dreamer." The coat Joseph wore gave them reason for hatred, but nothing raised their ire like the interpretations of his dreams. They could not point a finger at Christ - "which of you convinceth Me of sin?" (John 8:46)

15

- but His doctrine, His teaching, to them was insufferable. How like human beings, they rejoice in a healing Christ, a giving Christ, a model or example Christ, but not a teaching Christ.

The Lord's teaching was simple but not surface. It was informative and interesting, but when one heard Him it was to feel exposed before the eye of God. His teaching convinced Nicodemus that He was a teacher come from God, even although he was no mean teacher himself. His public preaching in the synagogue made a demon-possessed man cry out. It caused a chief publican to run and climb up a sycamore tree so that he might get a glimpse of Him. What the rulers and the religious leaders could not suffer was that His teaching exposed the nest of unclean birds which had been roosting in their hearts for centuries. The light was truly shining in the darkness. Either they allow it to find out every unclean corner, or they extinguish it. Thus we see the reason men had to slander Christ. They said "we be not born of fornication" (John 8:41), "He casteth out devils through Beelzebub" (Luke 11:15), "how knoweth this man letters, having never learned?" (John 7:15) - a slander to His religious education. They look at His coat, woven without seam; at His colleagues, at the colt on which He sat. Like Joseph how willingly He submitted to their barbarity.

Joseph was hated and envied

No trial is so fiery as when one is hated without a cause. The psalmist speaks of "they that hate me without a cause are more than the hairs of mine head" (Psalm 69:4). All the things which raise men's hatred against each other, were absent in Christ. High birth is often the subject of others' malice and spite. Opportunity in life and advantages cause the rich to envy. Arrogance and human assertiveness spawns hatred. The list is endless of things which give men reason for hatred and envy, but these were not found in Christ. None was so lowly born or had less advantage than Christ. His life was sought from His birth - He had to find asylum in Egypt because Judea had become an inquisition house. No arrogance or self-assertiveness marked Him as He grew up. He was a tender plant, sensitive to God's glory and mankind's misery. How could they hate One whose voice brought stability to deeply distressed manhood like the man from Gadara? Or whose virtue brought instant healing to the womanhood of the nation, like the woman afflicted with the issue of blood? The tenderness with which Christ approached the young maid who lay dead and, taking her hand and raising her up to life, tells of a compassion and sympathy unequalled in history; yet like Joseph He had to endure progressive hatred, ultimate shame, and deepest humiliation.

Joseph was stripped of his beautiful woven coat
That coat was provided at great cost to his father, and what joy it gave him to bestow it, but now Joseph is roughly handled and stripped. How his sensitive spirit must have felt all the pent up fury of their hearts. The Judgement Hall and Herod's Court, mad dogs (uncontrolled minds), wild bulls (ungovernable passions), men who know nothing of moderation, and others who knew nothing of mitigation, all are represented at the well's mouth in the desert and at the Lord's trial. Reuben is like Pilate - indecisive, Simon is representative of cruelty, Judah (Judas) representative of personal gain. In these scenes we behold the world as it was and as it is.

On the cross of Christ three languages were written up:

Hebrew	– the hypocrisy of the religious world;
Greek	– the philosophy of the cultured world;
Latin	– the tyranny of the military world.

He was stripped and shamed and every indignity heaped upon His holy manhood because His doctrine exposed each of these three powers, leaving no room but for repentance and complete and total submission to the truth as revealed in Jesus. I never read in Genesis of Joseph taking back one syllable of his disclosures or begging mercy or offering apologies; but like Him "who, when He was reviled, reviled not again; when He suffered, He threatened not" (1 Peter 2:23).

Joseph was sold

The brothers thought that they had seen the last of this pestilent fellow! "When shall He die, and His name perish?" (Psalm 41:5) I do not read that Joseph was ill-treated by the Ishmaelites who carried him down to Egypt. How strange that in the days of His flesh, the poor and unlearned had an ear for Christ, centurions had respect, and He was warmly respected for actions He did by people outside the nation of Israel. The twenty pieces of silver paid for him was the brothers' mercenary valuation of Joseph. I read nothing of the sale price in the Egyptian auction: we don't expect it. But to sell Joseph was to sell their God-sent messiah: "He sent a man before them, even Joseph" (Psalm 105:17). Our valuation of Christ is the gauge, the corner stone of every life, family and nation, not to speak of the church. It will determine our progress and future usefulness, and will be absolutely vital to our place in the kingdom. "You cannot be right in the rest if you do not think rightly of Him."

Joseph was falsely accused and tempted

All trials have links in the chain of divine providence. The sorest of all trials in Joseph's experience was in Potiphar's house. Trial has not always an ugly face. The wife of Potiphar was possibly very charming and highly skilled in the art of seduction. She never gave up or passed any opportunity to gain her objective. Joseph had no Bible, no Scripture, but so close were these trials to truth that God has included them in the sacred writings. The temptations of our Lord Jesus are a marvellous example to all humanity. He hungered forty days and afterwards - "command these stones be made bread" (Matt 4:3) – He overcame the bread test. "Cast Thyself down" (Matt 4:5) – He overcame the promotion test. Then He was offered a crown without a cross. Joseph came out of all this without a coat but retained intact his wholesome character. Our Lord's temptations proved how fit He was to be the sinless sacrifice upon the cross.

Joseph was silent in the face of slander

Note the silence of this man when his Egyptian master's wrath was unleashed upon him, and how in later life he never recalls it. Note the silence of our Lord in the face of His accusers even when His chief apostles deny Him; His look speaks volumes. He will answer whom He chooses to answer. Herod cannot make him speak, and He will address the High Priest only when necessary. Thieves revile, catcalls are shouted at Him from Skull-hill, but speak He will not. Mothers get a word from Him, also His own mother and John His friend, and a penitent thief draws from Him a promise on the verge of eternity. His agony of thirst is expressed, His forgiving heart is revealed, "Father, forgive them" (Luke 23:34). His finished work is announced, then His spirit commended to His Father. But injuries, wounds, indignities, mockery, shame and dishonour are borne silently:

> "Silent in Thine agony,
> Dying, crushed beneath the load,
> Of the wrath and curse of God."

Joseph serves both great and small

Potiphar and prisoner alike were served. What contrasting people came to Christ. Position, possessions, parentage meant nothing to Him. Joseph served the guilty and the guiltless. Christ never refused to come and dine when even thoughts and motives were clouded (Luke 7:36; 14:1). He will serve all: whether it is a nobleman's son or a

Syrophenician's daughter, whether as a one parent family or a full complement father-mother-daughter, or a widow with her only son, He will serve them all. He cleanses ten lepers and knows only one will return. How willingly and exhaustively (as at Sychar's well) but how impartially the blessed Lord served.

Joseph knew that God was with him

In all the seeming reverses in Joseph's life he lived with the daily consciousness that God was with Him, "who sweetened every bitter cup". What words escape our Lord's lips, "Father I knew that Thou hearest Me always" (John 11:42), and, "Jesus lifted up His eyes to heaven" (John 17:1). We have to close our eyes because of distractions but He alone could lift up His eyes to heaven, the only man on earth who knew unbroken communion. This was because in Him there was not a trace of Adam's sin; and when He preached God showed His approval by signs and miracles.

Joseph was the revealer of secrets

Here we have Joseph as the prophet before the world's greatest potentates. He has told the future of Israel; now he will tell the future to the Gentiles, albeit Israel cannot be severed from these dispensational matters. What heartbreak and sorrow this world could be spared if only they would obey the Lord's voice from the Holy Mount: "Hear ye Him" (Matt 17:5). Christ is greater than Israel's great prophets, Moses and Elijah; also the church's foremost pillars, Peter, James and John. The voice declares, "Hear ye Him"; hear what He says in relation to sin, to self, to Satan, to Israel, to the nations, about the future, about the coming, the rapture and manifestation. Hear His discourse on the tribulation and Jacob's trouble, of the indescribable horror of days when God's judgement shall fall and unmitigated wrath be poured out on a sin-loving, God-hating, rebellious world. Hear Him tell of the Antichrist, the false Prophet and of Satan himself, and their predicted doom. The Lord Jesus was the greatest prophetic teacher ever known. Joseph's predictions all came true. Christ's shall all be fulfilled to the jot and tittle: "a prophet shall the Lord your God raise up unto you of your brethren, like unto me; Him shall ye hear" (Acts 7:37).

Joseph became Egypt's wise administrator

"Can we find such a One as this is?" - true of Joseph and of Him who will rule "from the river to the ends of the earth". Everything is gathered up for God and for the good of man under His righteous administration.

Summary

With joy and profit we search these great typical teachings, which foreshadow our Lord Jesus Christ – this has been amply written upon by others. Suffice to say that on no fewer than thirty-seven occasions we have a striking resemblance between Joseph and our Lord Jesus Christ. It would be fair comment to say that Joseph is as close a picture of Christ as any, yet the observant reader will discover that on quite a number of occasions Joseph fails to answer to the antitype. Every type is only a type and must come short of Him who "did no sin" (1 Peter 2:22) and "knew no sin" (2 Cor 5:21) and "in Him is no sin" (1 John 3:5).

Dispensational truth in relation to Israel is also very evident in this narrative; for example seen in the rejection of Christ by His brethren, their subsequent selling of Him, their callous indifference in the face of revelation and also miracles, wonders, and signs; their linking with the Gentile nation to put Him to death, never thinking that "God hath made that same Jesus, whom ye have crucified, both Lord and Christ" (Acts 2:36). The span of time between His rejection and exaltation are portrayed with vividness in the life of Joseph, the important time factor between His crucifixion and His manifestation. His slowness to reveal Himself until true repentance is revealed and former wrongs righted, His succour of them through severe tribulation conditions (to preserve life) is most significant and absorbing and instructive. But in this study our exercise is to show the progress, patience, devotion and spirituality of this beautiful character called Joseph.

CHAPTER 2

Joseph and his Birth

(Gen 30:22-25)

The name of Joseph, whether referred to in the Old or New Testament, is always held very dear. Possibly this is because his youthfulness is so pure, his desires so noble, his character so developed, or his patience so excellent in one so young. We generally link his beginnings with Genesis 37:1 when he was seventeen years of age, and possibly at this age was the true beginning of his experience with God. In later life he would learn the circumstances that had brought his father into Laban's house in Padanaram, of his labours in the heat by day and frost by night, of the treachery of his grandfather in giving Leah in the place of his loved mother Rachel. Jacob was to see the other side of the family coin, Rebecca on one side and her brother Laban on the other.

How precious to see that Joseph was the subject of his mother's prayers, albeit I say prayers and not patience, yet God remembered Rachel. Life had proved a sad disappointment: she waited patiently for seven years for Jacob, only to find in the end that she had been supplanted and her sister been given, and she possibly found herself the laughing stock of all the neighbourhood. Jacob's anger at Laban was never to be relieved and Rachel's respect was never again given to her father, so far as we may read on the surface of this domestic sequel. A father's planning brought lifelong and weary contention into the daily experiences in Jacob's household. Jacob's first and official wife was not loved and only suffered to remain; Rachel, loved and delighted in, her face and form most beautiful to behold, and yet fretful and envious. What situations parents can put their children into by scheming and planning! Using one's children for one's own advantage must be very shallow and mean.

To add to Joseph's mother's trials, Leah began to bear children, thus adding further aggravation to the home experience. Leah, Joseph's aunt, was sensitive to her rejection, and in the naming of her sons her whole experience in life comes into view. Contention and competition to win Jacob's affections are not hid from us, and the incident of the mandrakes (love apples) show us the height of this. These contentions should have brought Rachel to where later Hannah came – to seek God's face quietly. Such words as "God remembered Rachel" (Gen 30:22), show that He had mercy on her. Her husband was grieved when she asked, "Give me children or else I die" (Gen 30:1). It is very important to note that she did die at the birth of her second child. God notes rash prayers as well as rash vows (as Jephthah's). Amid her seeming lack of patience and great matrimonial misery, and seemingly not quite delivered from idols, relics and keepsakes, yet God remembered Rachel. We cannot but be touched by a very pitiful God who not only does not mark iniquities, but also has compassion on the ignorant, and sees every distraught domestic circumstance, knowing we are but dust. Spurgeon said, "Would to God we would remember." If Paul advises giving honour as unto the weaker vessel, we see in Rachel weakness but not wickedness, infirmity but not iniquity.

Joseph was born in Syria. His birth was delayed to teach his mother discipline, to bring her through the school of patience (she did not graduate with Honours!), to awaken a grateful heart. His name Joseph, meaning "He will add", was prophetic. Rachel had revelation that another son would be born. It was at the birth of Joseph that Jacob felt stirrings for his own country. Births and burials seem to play a great part in the movements of these men of faith. The beginning of life and its cessation seemed to cause them to pause and consider their position. When Joseph was born his father was very poor. One could never have foreseen that from this poor set of circumstances - a penniless shepherd, two wives, two concubines, then a large family of sons – would become a great nation: nothing in Padanaram to call his own, nothing yet to leave his sons. Ten times Laban had changed his wages, and knowing Laban, we cannot believe it would be upward. Under such oppression, and Jacob fighting for an existence, Joseph was reared. What he would lack in luxuries, his mother's love would amply supply; what he missed in delicacies, he had in motherly devotion. These were the experiences in Padanaram, with want and hand-to-mouth existence, yet Jacob could speak of "the God which fed me all my life long" (Gen 48:15).

Joseph was only a lad when his father had some of his deeper experiences with God. He was to grow up with his father, a broken, leaning man, but acknowledged by God as a Prince, and given a new title 'Israel'. He had the experience of meeting Esau, the uncle who preferred the temporal in place of the spiritual, who lived for time and not for eternity. His father shielded him from the fierceness of this red man of the earth. This lesson should be clearly taught that it is the responsibility of spiritual parents to shield their families from every influence that would spoil them.

Moses' mother shielded him as long as she could. When she could no longer hide him, she covered him in the ark of bulrushes and even after that she only put him by the river's brink, not into the mainstream, and then posted Miriam to watch over the child. What a lesson for parents when children have to go elsewhere to further education or be trained in skills, or even just a change of job. Do we inquire about accommodation? Do we find out the whereabouts of a spiritual home for our young ones? This is a crucial time in their lives and they need to know someone whom they can

25

trust and more so, confide in. What a work here for spiritual women and what a mighty work have women done in having opened their homes, hearths and hearts. Many today are thankful for the love, advice, and hospitality given in homes which were opened to them.

Thus we have briefly traced Joseph's birth and early experiences as far as Scripture permits. Possibly his hidden years are not accounted for until God takes dealings with him and he becomes the vessel of divine revelation. The age of Joseph when his mother died is not easy to ascertain, but the loss of his mother must have played a great part in his human development. Possibly had she lived she would have spared him from the many problems he encountered with his brothers, but this also would have been counter-productive to the purpose of God that was to be wrought out. While the circumstances of life were seemingly against him and capable of making him sour, yet the very opposite was the case in his life.

Joseph, the seventeen year old (Gen 37:1)

Joseph the seventeen year old now enters that sphere of life where he has to work in close proximity to others, leave home, and labour in the fields. Thus he enters the "adversity phase" of his experience. We will all be anxious to know how he fares when away from home and holy influences and parental constraints. In these seventeen years his father has become wealthy, his brothers had become crooked and cruel, and his sister Dinah's behaviour had caused tragedy in a whole township. His father was well able to keep his son at home and could have spoiled him with parental indulgence. But Jacob knows that life without testing and burden bearing and labour and weariness is a pampered life. Idleness in young people is the nurse of other vices.

Though of meaner birth, pride was still prevalent in the brothers' hearts. A mean birth should keep us humble and a high birth should make us grateful. At seventeen years, involved in daily toil, labouring with the meanest of the concubines' sons, feeding the flock, taking his responsibility; all this is a very wonderful introduction to behold in one so young. We also see it in Israel's future king, and see it in Him who went down to Nazareth and was subject unto His parents; wonderful to see the vessel of divine choice as the carpenter's son, and then on His own account, the carpenter. See also another choice soul in some back street in Tarsus or some large loft with the name plate 'Tentmaker'.

The only thing beneath a child of God to do is to sin. Thus Jacob's generation is to commence with Joseph (v.2), not with any of the other sons. Sin had come into Jacob's household in a very public way. Reuben has shamed his father's bed. This same sin was re-enacted at Corinth in the most gifted church of the New Testament. Simeon and Levi murdered men under the pretext of zeal, but their father said that their wrath was cruel, and he felt the shame of Shechem. Anger and self-will puts one far from the line of blessing. Judah sins in chapter 38, and shows the base hypocrisy of the human heart, and when found out he has to confess, "She hath been more righteous than I." (Gen 38:26)

These matters in Joseph's family add value and credibility to this whole history. Nothing is to be glossed over. Joseph's intimate relationship with his father goes beyond the weak suggestion of parental partiality; not that this matter is not important to correct, for any instance of this can never be removed from the family mind. It was not a case of "Jacob's pet". Jacob could not suppress his joy in Joseph. All the others had disappointed him and brought his grey hair to the grave. His sons were habitually evil. He had no confidence in their word or transactions. But it was joy to have someone like Joseph who answered to his spiritual longings, who saw things from God's standpoint, and who saw the awfulness of sin against God, who could converse on subjects beyond camel's carcasses and costs, who saw into the future and saw God had a purpose and a place for him. He could dwell on these things and he knew his father's thoughts about matters. He grieved over his brothers' doings. The gift of the many-coloured coat was a preferment to Joseph of the first-born's place. But in the nature of the coat of many colours, Jacob was saying, "All I have longed for in my family and have not seen, I have found here. Joseph has filled the deepest joys of my heart." How beautiful that in Christ, the Father has found a blessed answer to all that He longed for, and how precious that we, as His children, can answer to this in affording pleasure to God as the graces of Christ are manifest in us. This preferment will bring joy to Jacob, but the sweet taste he enjoys is sour in his sons' mouths. These men are carnal and undisciplined, and cannot or will not bring joy to their father.

What then is our motive in life? What was theirs? If they did not please their father, they must have lived to please themselves. That position meant much to them is clearly proved by their words, "Shalt thou indeed reign over us?" (Gen 37:8). The deeds they transacted exposed their covetous hearts, the sins they committed gave evidence of unbridled lust. What then was that motive in life? - it was self.

The sequel to the coat given by his father, and his love expressed, is that hatred develops; then there is the repeating of that first scene outside Eden's garden. Whenever Abel pleases God, Cain hates him and cannot speak peaceably with him. When once we become carnal, cruelty will follow. This struggle and fight that is the inevitable experience of the spiritual man has never lessened as the dispensations have passed, until we read at the close of the age "Michael and his angels fought against the dragon" (Rev 12:7). Even Gog and Magog raise their ugly head at the end of one thousand years of righteous peace (Rev 20:8). They are subjugated, but the power of evil must never be underestimated. How sad to find in the chosen family of Jacob there is only one with a mind for holy things and a sensitivity about sin. How strange that even in the best ordered assemblies these features crop up like old leprosy. If hatred exists, ears will be closed to revelation (dreams), and murderous thoughts will germinate. His brethren (half-brothers) were evil and contentious. No details of their evil are given, but if the past history of Reuben and Judah (moral), and of Simeon and Levi (cruelty and bestiality) is any guide, we are left with little scope for leniency.

We have no reason to think that Joseph took any pleasure in carrying bad tidings to his father. What he did was a charitable and brotherly deed, though not appreciated. How sad when everyone else knows except the parents and those so closely involved. Often, had matters been brought to light sooner, sins could have been avoided. This is not an excuse for talebearers; this is a matter for delicate lips and for those with a loving concern for all involved. To know of sin and to hide it is to be party to it. Parents should not be angry when those like Joseph come with matters of concern, but should feel indebted to persons who assist them by prudent and accurate information. Great caution must be taken in this ministry lest we bring upon ourselves the reproach of interference in other men's matters. As an aside, it would be wise for all to note that when even the best of men with the best intentions give judgements on other peoples' matters, very rarely do they come from the case without the smell of the fire upon them. Thus, this matter was a family matter, for father, sons and brothers. Family matters are best resolved in that sphere.

Joseph grieved for his father's testimony. This is the only reason for bringing back the report. Shallow interpretation has suggested that Joseph was a talebearer – an old Scots word is a clipe! He spoke to his father because they would not listen to his remonstrations – "and could not speak peaceably unto him" (Gen 37:4). Joseph goes to his father as the last pillar of authority in the family. Jacob's affection and Joseph's integrity stimulate their hatred.

Other peoples' happiness and acceptance is often gall to others. The envious man scarcely knows what a cycle of events he sets in motion against himself. He sets out to ruin others and in the process ruins himself. The fruits of this are deadly; will cause endless sorrow, tears and grey hairs; will bring cleavages between families, neighbours and friends; it will ease a personal tension, but it will cause world-wide havoc. "Jealousy is cruel as the grave" (Song of Songs 8:6); it is the father of strife and vainglory, it will take away the beauty of any life, "it is rottenness to the bones" (Prov 14:30). "Who can stand before envy?" (Prov 27:4). The first seeds of this showed in their attitude; the next in their words, "could not speak peaceably"; finally in their hands - the intended murder, then slavery, and the selling for twenty pieces of silver. "Whosoever hateth his brother is a murderer" (1 John 3:15).

In the midst of these most difficult and painful daily experiences, God reveals Himself to Joseph. What a consolation! Just at the moment when the fire was heated and the lion's mouth open, God came in with holy consolations in the form of revelation. This was to be the stimulus and strength for greater trial and the ultimate lifting-up of his head. God comes in at the most crucial moments and reveals or releases. He shall not try you more than you are able to bear, "but will with the temptation make a way to escape, that ye may be able to bear it" (1 Cor 10:13). We see this in Abraham and the ram, David in the wood of Ziph, Peter at night in the prison, and Paul in the basket. While this was a consolation to Joseph, it was a revelation and a prophecy concerning his whole family.

In the purpose of God, Joseph was to be the central figure, "My sheaf arose, and also stood upright" (Gen 37:7). Dignity and glory were his allotted portion. His brother's sheaves all made obeisance to his sheaf. The interpretation was very distinct – it involved food, life, existence, the field. It shall be known in this way. Joseph was exalted, his brothers submissive. The dream was doubled and the vision was next in the heavens. Sun, moon and stars bowed down to him; the doubling of the dream was to certify the validity of it all. Blessings earthly and heavenly, temporal and spiritual ,were ahead for this family. Would they now grasp them, change their evil ways, become single-eyed, and acknowledge Joseph as the man approved of God?

Joseph as yet did not know that his dreams would have fulfilment in another man's dreams, in a set of circumstances quite foreign to himself. God has a purpose for the nations (Egypt), but these shall come to pass via the medium of Israel, and not so much the sons of Jacob. What a confidence these revelations would have been when the famine came. How good of God to leave on record for us His prophetic program so that when it comes to pass, we are not at a loss, but calmly wait its fulfilment. Joseph's brethren, however, will not give up the principle of the first man. Blessing is not in Reuben but in Joseph the second (firstborn of Rachel). Men hold on to the first Adam. God's invested authority is in the last Adam.

Joseph's transparency in telling his brothers the dreams (Gen 37:5-9)

The first dream he told to his brothers and the second he possibly told at home in the presence of all. The contempt of his brothers, "shall *we*" and "to *thee*", take us to other stories where history repeats itself: David and Eliab, Saul and David ("this stripling"). One feels in the second dream that the father is trying to pour oil on troubled waters, "Shall I and thy mother bow down?" (v.10). Jacob here may have given his sons room to doubt Joseph's dream. He seems to throw cold water on the young man's revelations. Many a parent, to appease his undisciplined family, has belittled the exercises of a spiritual son. He does with Joseph what he should have done years ago with the others – rebuked them. The sin of

Eli later on is that "he restrained them not" (1 Sam 3:13). Samuel's sons and David's son are a glowing example of this matter.

If only eye salve had been on their eyes, how precious these revelations would have been, and how respectfully they would have faced the coming famine, even though it was twenty years away. His father's prophetic and personal experience with God caused him to observe the saying (v.11). An important issue is at stake here. God has spoken, He has repeated His message (two dreams). The hearers' attitude is divinely recorded – "They envied him" (v.11). They turned their backs on revealed truth. Jacob observed, gave it serious consideration. Twenty years would pass before its fulfilment, but what did they care? They were like their uncle Esau, they lived for the present. If only we could grasp that God has a purpose. Christ is the central figure, and our happiness and future are dependent on how we position ourselves around Him. Oh the misery and heartbreak of the self-willed child of God! Their attitude to Joseph was their attitude to revelation, to truth, to invested authority. They could not see the corn and the blessing because of their envy.

One of the most disquieting aspects of these dreams was that the brothers did not need to be told the interpretation, they saw the meaning immediately. It took no special explaining. Herein is the disaster area of our lives. We know God has spoken, we know God is right, we know His wisdom is supreme, we know He will never go back on His word. In one of the best known passages in the Bible, Matthew tells us that the wise men came, seeking, and were told from Scripture where the Lord Jesus would be born (Matt 2:5). They search, find, give, rejoice and return, but none in Jerusalem joined them to find "Emmanuel - God with us" (Matt 1:23). Later they will search and slay, because they could not suffer the thought of a rival; they would not come and bow. The Lord Jesus in brief words said, "If ye love Me, keep (obey) My commandments" (John 14:15). God has given very clear revelation in the epistles in regard to relationships: "Be ye kind one to another" (Eph 4:32); "Be ye not unequally yoked together with unbelievers" (2 Cor 6:14); "Be ye holy; for I am holy" (1 Pet 1:16).

Here are men who twice hear what God has to say and perceive it not, but double their sin by the black malice they show to the child who brought the message. Who were they to question divine prerogatives? None of them was fit material for God to speak through. Thus they rebelled against His sovereign choice, for Joseph was like Him who was of another order, who came from above.

CHAPTER 3

Joseph and his Brethren

(Gen 37)

We have just concluded our consideration of Joseph from his birth until he is seventeen years old.

Jacob kept him at home while his brethren went with the flocks, so as to spare him from the constant antagonism, which they could not now hide. But being in Shechem caused Jacob further grief. He would never forget the cruelty of his sons. No sorrow equals the disappointment in one's own family, and yet the godly of all generations seem to have been afflicted with it. Ishmael shall mock Isaac, Esau shall despise what Jacob most loves, Esau shall marry those who grieve his parents, Isaac and Rebecca. Eli will suffer a blow in his two sons, as Aaron did before him, then Samuel's sons walk not in their father's steps. Then David's four sons, Amnon, Absalom, Adonijah, and the child born to Bathsheba, all give us further examples. This has been so often repeated that the tears of God's people are never ceasing over such matters. While the prodigal son seemingly was a single man, most of those formerly listed were married, and no age is exempt. Jacob's trials with Laban were as nothing compared with those of his devious household.

Did Jacob feel Joseph's presence would help at Shechem? Whatever the reason, we see submission in a son to do his father's bidding. We see Joseph leaving the vale of Hebron alone - twenty years will pass before they embrace again. Many weary, lonely days will pass, salt tears will be shed, hair will grow whiter, there will be pain for them both; for the purpose of God is performed through pain. We consider our Lord Jesus "who for the joy that was set before Him endured the cross, despising the shame, and is set down at the right hand of the throne of God" (Heb 12:2).

> *"By meekness and defeat*
> *He won the mead and crown;*
> *Trod all His foes beneath His feet*
> *By being trodden down."*

In his journey to meet his brethren he does not find them where he expected. They had moved from Shechem to Dothan. Possibly fearing some retaliation for the Shechem massacre, these men were restless. Those of an evil disposition can never settle: "the wicked are like the troubled sea, when it cannot rest, whose waters cast up mire and dirt" (Isaiah 57:20). When Joseph found them not at Shechem, he was informed that they had gone to Dothan. How natural it would have been for him to return and honestly say he could not find them, but the heart of the true shepherd was in him and he sought till he found them. For all his trouble he got little or no thanks. His honest endeavours were ill rewarded.

Contrary to the opinion of eminent scholars and spiritual writers, Joseph is not a perfect type. Here we find him "wandering in the field". This could never be said of our blessed Lord – "Jesus knowing that all things . . ." (John 19:28). Oftentimes guidance is near if a questing spirit is within. As he approached their encampment, they saw him coming. They begin to mock and sneer: "Behold this dreamer cometh" (v.19). His dress was a mote in their eye; his dreams added fuel to the fire of envy; his disclosure as to their submission to him was unbearable. They could not bow to Joseph, but they could stoop to murder. They seemed to be at home scheming and deceiving. What a sight to see this comely youth stripped of his lovely coat! This is what they thought of their father's choice and his wisdom! On previous occasions they used only their tongues, but now their hands take delight in stripping him. Though stripped, yet they cannot bear his presence nor avoid his eyes looking into theirs. (Likewise in the trial of our Lord Jesus, they blindfolded Him.) They put Joseph in a pit or some disused well. They showed their hatred to their father now, and they put his son out of sight. When envy rules, pity is absent. When men become carnal, opposing the mind of God, they then become cruel. This scene was never to be erased from their minds, "the anguish of his soul" (Gen 42:21). What a solemn sight at that well! Feelingless brethren with murderous intent!

But God's thoughtfulness was not missing; there was no water in the pit. God mingles mercy with our suffering. When Benaiah was in the pit with a lion, it was a time of snow - most difficult conditions. When Jeremiah was in his dungeon, he sank in the mire. Both of these men were experienced servants of God and could bear such difficulties. But God tempers the wind to spare the shorn lamb. Reuben, the firstborn who has many faults (unstable), sets out to deliver the lad, but waits too long (indecision). In the meantime Ishmaelites are on the horizon, and Judah, who will show a prophetic picture of the nation of Israel's nature which will come out so unerringly in Judas Iscariot, says "What profit is it if we slay our brother?" (v.26).

The steps they took were very ordinary to them - no grief or hesitation were shown:

the coat stripped - they renounced his birthright;
starved him - they relinquished brotherhood;
they sold him - they refused human rights;
they slay a kid - they cover their sin in an innocent's blood.

Notice their guile in the blood-covered coat. They say to their father, "Know now if this be thy son's coat or no" (v.32); not "our brother" but "thy son". The grief that this incident brought to their father was so intense Jacob longed to die.

Here he was with these ten men and not one of them had his confidence. The only one who understood him and appreciated holy things was seemingly gone. His sons and daughters-in-law rise up to comfort him, but guilty men make very poor comforters. Let families beware that they add not to the number of their parents' grey hairs! Jacob was growing old and this was a very heavy burden. The brothers of Joseph were so smug, so sure; "what shall become of his dreams?" (v.20). But they reckoned without God. They meant it for evil, but God meant it for good.

The lesson of these incidents is so clear: "Oh what a tangled web we weave, when first we practise to deceive!"

CHAPTER 4

Joseph the Bondslave

(Gen 39 - 41)

The scene changes and now we find Joseph in the land of Egypt, a land of culture and a settled, stable life which was so different from Joseph's nomadic experience. It must have been very humiliating to be auctioned in the slave market. One so sensitive as Joseph, yes, one who had been so loved and so favoured of God as to have His counsel revealed - to be handled, speculated upon, bid for like a beast. But nothing could hide the beauty and purity of this lovely soul. No circumstance can rob the spiritual man of the endowed heavenly look. Moses, descending the mountain having been in the presence of God "wist not that the skin of his face shone" (Exod 34:29); those in the council looking upon Stephen as he suffered a most barbarous death "saw his face as it had been the face of an angel" (Acts 6:15). The man of God's purpose can stand the look of any crowd. "Who before Pontius Pilate witnessed a good confession" (1 Tim 6:13).

In the slave market that day was Potiphar. He was very near to the king, possibly Chief of the Police or Minister for Internal Affairs. The steps to the throne of Egypt begin here. It is most moving to observe the four slaves who altered Israel's destiny, yea were to affect all the generations to come; for God's purpose is linked with Israel and blessing is in store for those who bless them, and cursing for those who curse them. (1) Joseph's slavery was to exalt him, and in that honoured capacity he would preserve life. (2) Moses was a slave in Egypt and he would deliver, and by his works (the

Pentateuch) guide Israel by the law, and bring them into nearer relationship with God. The world has never valued the contribution Moses made to life's dignity. (3) Daniel also was a slave in Babylon and saw a number of dynasties rise and fall, and God gave him knowledge of those things which would befall His people in the latter times. (4) Esther is our final example who, though a queen, finds herself at the mercy of an edict deceitfully planned by Haman, the archenemy of the Jews in that far-off day. How purposefully, and self-sacrificially through fasting, she sets about the operation of delivering her people. Through patience she won that deliverance for her people. Therefore let no-one say, I am low or limited in usefulness. They all in their day served their own generation well.

Potiphar's house

From the dignity of sonship and firstborn status (the coat) he now takes up the servant's livery. I read not of refining or of a disgruntled attitude. He begins to serve Potiphar the way he served his father. He was possibly unused to city life, yet he seems to have a versatility about him which adapts to the will of God for him. He serves with alacrity, in an alien land. Bowing to the task before him he finds himself blessed of God and honoured by men. I read not of many words, but deeds; and soon promotion is given. Dignity, integrity and suffering add something to a man, and bring him to the point of contentment. So great was his master's trust that he set him over all his household and outside interests. Potiphar knew not what he had in the house, but his business interests took an upturn and the Lord blessed his house "for Joseph's sake" (Gen 39:5). Here was a man diligent in this limited sphere, and taking control of this household. He first had learned to control himself, then this household. Soon he will control the prison, and finally all the nations shall come under his control, but at this point He was learning to be faithful in little.

Fleeing youthful lust

No man whom the Lord has blessed and who has been given a degree of ability, can expect peaceful days forever. Nothing can be so difficult as to be in close confinement with others, and especially those of the opposite sex. Joseph would seem to have been very handsome, and his private life with God would put an added grace and dignity upon him. The culture and forwardness of civilisation in Egypt at this time was beyond question, but here its women folk are depicted in this society lady. She entertained a very low concept of marriage. She thought nothing of deceiving her husband, and she was driven by the insatiable desires of lust. She may have been high born but her language is the language of the harlot, "Lie with me" (Gen 39:7). Temptations of this kind often arise daily and are very difficult to overcome. These sins of the flesh, which if succumbed to are sins against the body, are very difficult to get over, and seem to haunt the mind.

Joseph's position was difficult, not wanting to offend the wife of his trusting master, and yet the moment has to come when he makes his position absolutely clear. He will deal with every overture in its context, but the trap is set, the house is empty, the offer is made, and only God can give special help in those times. He has suffered, having been stripped and sold; now a seductress invites him. What trying situations the choicest of souls have found themselves in, neither seeking, planning or wanting it; but unlike Reuben, Judah, and Dinah, he decides to flee, irrespective of the consequences. He does the right thing by God and leaves the outcome with God. He plainly is in a situation where talking, remonstrating, reasoning are useless. He must get himself out. He reminds his temptress of her husband's trust. But he puts moral living on a plain hitherto unknown - "and sin against God" (Gen 39:9). No written commands condemned him, no eyes of superiors were upon him, no family restrictions were present; just one over-riding consideration – "sinning against God". Sin had a bad taste in Joseph's mouth; he could not swallow it. Like Job, he "eschewed evil" (spat it out), would not allow it into his digestive system to poison his whole manhood.

Let it be clearly understood and taught that adultery is wickedness, irrespective of modern standards. It is the greatest contributor to broken hearts and homes and lives. It was the reason for Samson's locks being shorn and his eyes put out; the reason for David's lovely life having a dark shadow which followed him to the grave. Joseph now leaves his coat in her hands. It has been so ably remarked upon but worth repeating that "he left his coat but not his character". He could get another coat but not another character. Thus a second coat has come off the shoulders of Joseph, the first with violence, the second voluntarily. While he flees, he does not run away. He awaits his master, he will stand trial, he will give an account of his stewardship. Potiphar's wife relates her account of the story, blaming Joseph for assault, blaming her husband for bringing "an Hebrew (in how short a space his family had become known) to mock us". The master's indignation knows no bounds and he possibly never gave Joseph a moment for explanation. What an education is this! - misunderstood by his brethren, now misrepresented by his master's wife! It is one of the great wonders of this story that his master did not slay him. Was it only divine intervention, or did Potiphar know his own wife and 'for face' assayed to put away Joseph? Putting him into the prison where the king's prisoners were kept was possibly a cover. No one would expect him to be put there!

Suffering for righteousness' sake

The lies of his seductress, the wrath of his trusting master and the loss of his favoured position, were all calculated to incite anger and revenge, but we are now to behold a man of a different order, yea a man of excellent spirit in the prison. It is in the many phases of life that character is truly formed.

God wants us for His glory, but He means to develop in us likeness to Christ. For Joseph, this will take many forms - family trials, commercial matters, the humiliation of being made to feel as nothing, misrepresented, then finally by his master misjudged.

He will be fitted out, or rather ill-fitted now with prison garb. How will he accept life's reverses? How will the will of God be wrought out here? So restrictive, so monstrous, so boring, but no sooner is he incarcerated than he begins to serve. What is this? He has raised moral thinking to majestic heights, now he will put menial tasks onto an altitude never seen before. To do the ordinary every day tasks with a measure of contentment is true elevation: "Godliness with contentment is great gain" (1 Tim 6:6). This was so far removed from his dreams of corn and sheaves and supremacy, far from sun and moon and stars and God's intended glory for Him. This matter of Joseph's service here is for the uplifting of everyone who might feel that ordinary life has no part in God's economy. Ashes had to be taken regularly from God's altar where the ascending offerings were burnt. Few understand, nor will they learn, that our Lord's life up to about thirty years old was filled with service and toil. Doing daily business with a most awkward people, a very price-conscious people, a very money-orientated people, yet among the weeds, the barren and shrivelled of Israel's society, He wrought and served, and could say, "Which of you convinceth Me of sin?" (John 8:46). There were no short cuts in His work, no price fixing and then additional bills, no shoddy workmanship, no inferior material.

Joseph's position now was to be numbered with transgressors. It is interesting to see that in this side of the prison at least, two of the three prisoners were innocent. It is most moving to see how observant of expressions Joseph was. He had lived with ten very strange mixtures, his own brethren. He became aware of moods, looks and depressions. Envy and jealousy have a disposition of their own. Who can stand against them? "Why look ye so sadly today?" (Gen 40:7). Joseph was conscious something was amiss. The butler and the baker, for thus the two notable prisoners are named, had had a very disturbed night, both had dreamed. The butler was first to tell his dream. Some reason must first be given as to why they were there at all. Surely when people rise to such positions in this great Egyptian society they would never imagine they would end up in jail. (But none of us can be sure of anything in this life except the promises God has vouchsafed in His Holy Word.) That someone had attempted to poison the king is the most reasonable solution one can offer. Both these men had closeness to the king's food and drink; therefore they came under suspicion.

The butler, who in another passage of scripture (Neh 1:11) was called a cupbearer, told Joseph his dream. The grapes, his hand openly squeezing them into the cup before the king's eyes, seemed to suggest openness and transparency of dealings, and the interpretation of his dream had a very happy ending. Joseph tells the butler the source of all interpretation, and then he proceeds to tell him in detail the meaning of his dream. He prophesies freedom and exaltation, and then adds a very pathetic plea to the butler. For the first time he tells part of his story, his being sold, but omitting to say who sold him. He tells his innocence but never names his master or his temptress, showing a remarkable control over his spirit. His choice of words is informative and enlightening, for he names only the wrong, but not the wrongdoers. No wonder the apostle Paul commends "the grace of our Lord Jesus Christ be with your spirit". Three times he desires this: Galatians 6:18 - when the effects of Judaism had caused biting and devouring in Galatia, it would need a spirit like Christ's to live there; 2 Timothy 4:22 - "The Lord Jesus Christ be with thy spirit" - in the face of coming apostasy (v.3) the presence of Christ indwelling would be needed to aid one's spirit; Philemon 25, when Philemon is asked to take back his erring servant, or brother (v.16) it would take a very considerable draught of the grace of our Lord Jesus to aid his spirit also.

The chief baker, when he saw the interpretation was good, offered to tell his dream. His dream, like the butler's, was in keeping with his calling. The numeral three is again employed. The baskets were white, they appeared clean, but the baskets were on his head, the topmost being open to the elements and the poisonous birds could foul the King's meat. Thus was established the carelessness of the baker and his lack of vigilance to protect his master. He allowed foreign elements to touch his master's diet. Joseph's prophecy pronounces death. What a message is this; to one he promises life and honour and exaltation, the other death and everlasting contempt.

What a solemn gospel is preached in this prison. Let us, like the butler, take the provision of God, the grapes as a picture of the blood, and bring it before the Throne. It is all the Throne requires, it needs no more. "The blood of Jesus Christ His son cleanses from all sin" (1 John 1:7). So many, like the baker, are hoping for a good end to a shadowy past; also hoping that their bakemeats will be accepted, a picture of man's shaping, artistry and decorations. But it can all be carried on the head in three tiers: "the lust of the flesh, and the lust of the eyes, and the pride of life" (1 John 2:16).

A very great lesson is before us. How humbly Joseph served these men, yet when the moment of truth about their future came, he told them faithfully the outcome of their lives. We too are called to serve men, and often in congenial circumstances. Are we as faithful? Are we afraid to lose face for Christ? But Joseph had been faithful in his father's house, he had been faithful in his master's house, he will now be faithful in the prison house. We cannot avoid seeing how mature this man has become. He is now about twenty seven years of age, he has had a vast experience of God and life, he has been accepted and rejected, misunderstood and misrepresented, has suffered for righteousness sake, he knows how to abound and now knows how to be abased. The continuity of the Lord's presence, "the Lord was with Joseph" (Gen 39:2,3,21,23), gave him acceptance. It is one of the cherished things in life to see men of God who have known the presence of the Lord in freshness and power.

It was a very bitter thing to behold his prophecy come true and for him not to profit immediately by it. In the two years after this the butler forgot him. It is possibly then that the iron entered into his soul. Twenty-eight years of age, handsome, prosperous, accepted, with remarkable ability whether in commerce or domestic affairs, to languish in a prison, circumscribed, no outlet for his talents - but God was putting the thorn into his flesh, because he had had an abundance of revelation. God in His character of refiner knows what the end product will be. He knows how much dross still requires consuming. This could possibly explain many of the weary days of waiting. His asking the butler to "think on me when it shall be well with thee" (Gen 40:14) is so very natural and forgivable, but God's purpose will use this man's offices on another day. The butler is restored and blessed yet he forgets. How conveniently we put out of mind the good that others lavish upon us! and yet we cannot or will never forget any indiscretion done to us! But forgetfulness can have serious consequences. "The wicked shall be turned into hell, and all the nations that forget God" (Psalm 9:17). We also court misery when we look into the mirror of God's Word and go away forgetting what manner of persons we are (James 1:24). What sadness and grief would be avoided if we "communicate and forget not" (Heb 13:16). Forgetfulness like the butler's is not a lapse, it is a vice. The word of the Lord by Joseph to the baker came to pass. What a solemn lesson in this first book of the Bible: God's promises and God's pronouncement shall both come to pass. Let poor sinners who perchance may read this book be aware, "God is not a man that He should lie" (Num 23:19), God will not change. Time is the only factor between you and an angry

God. Take heed; find rest and peace in God's provision, the blood of His own dear Son.

Joseph at thirty years of age

The mention of his age at this time is instructive (Gen 41:46). He is now a mature man with a vast experience. He was brought up in Syria, he had lived and wrought in Canaan, he had fallen to the level of a slave, yet had enjoyed and proved his ability as a steward among the upper classes in Potiphar's house, and he has had considerable time and conversation with two very senior Court Officials, the chief butler and baker. We may note three things:

His ministry had been mocked   - the dreams;
His morality has been questioned   - Potiphar's wife;
His helpfulness has been forgotten   - the butler.

Now this slave was going to alter destiny. All his trials did not make him cynical or sour, no root of bitterness was in his heart, his experience had made him soft, touched, broken and contrite. He must have felt like his father, "all these things are against me" (Gen 42:36), but little did his father or he know all these things instead were for him. William Cowper, that most spiritual of hymn writers, said:

> *"Judge not the Lord by feeble sense*
> *But trust Him for His grace;*
> *Behind a frowning providence*
> *He hides a smiling face.*
>
> *His purposes will ripen fast,*
> *Unfolding every hour;*
> *The bud may have a bitter taste*
> *But sweet will be the flower."*

His past experience with God and with others will make

him unawed before Pharaoh. Pharaoh, king of Egypt has two dreams. Joseph has altogether three sets of dreams to interpret. The first is at home with his family; the second is in confinement with the prisoners; the third and last will be linked with a palace. Before coming to these dreams and their implications let us see how God reveals himself to Joseph.

God is so condescending and gracious to reveal His mind to a seventeen-year-old in a field, to Zacharias in the holy place (John Baptist's father), to a maiden in a peasant's home in Nazareth, to Peter on a roof top at Joppa, and to Paul in a Roman prison. "Where'er we seek Him He is found and every place is hallowed ground."

The dreams of this despotic ruler are, to say the least, baffling to the natural man. That God intends to send him a message is clear, but God also intends to educate this man. He will learn his own futility in understanding the deep things of God, and also his own ignorance. In Egypt, this forward-looking civilisation and advanced culture, God will show Pharaoh, its representative head, that he is a very limited man. The King calls all his wise men, and their variety is noteworthy, so that no problem will ever want proper attention. But cows eating cows, and corn eating corn, is beyond the scope of all the accumulated brains of Egypt. Few Christians have learned that the world's wisdom is one of the main enemies of the revelation of God. Paul who could boast more wisdom than most, had learned that "the world by wisdom knew not God" (1 Cor 1:21). We must beware that an educated ministry does not take the place of a Spirit-filled ministry, albeit we honour everyone who has an education and has used it with modesty in a spiritual sphere.

The court of Egypt is in turmoil; the magicians and wise men cannot interpret. The suave, plausible magicians cannot assuage the wrath of the monarch - the sentence of death is passed on them for failing to fulfil the reason for their existence. The butler of Joseph's past experience now has a seeming jolt of memory. How strange and convenient our memories are, especially when we are near crisis point! We remember everything and everyone we can use to advantage. The butler addresses himself to his lord: "I do remember my faults this day" (Gen 41:9). He begins to go over his experience, the prison, the accusation, the dreams, the young Hebrew, the interpretation, the restoration of himself and the death of his colleague, the baker. He called his lapse of memory "my faults". It is strange when we find faults in others they are sins, but in ourselves we call them faults. How protective we are of ourselves, how harsh with others!

The moment of release has come for Joseph. He is sent for and brought hastily before the king. Before he appears he gives attention to his personal appearance - he shaves himself. Like a Nazarite who has accomplished his vow he has been a separate man, quite distinct and distinguished, separate from his brethren. A new era has begun; he is now going to taste the wine of joy. He has known adversity; having been tempted to impurity, he will now be trusted with prosperity. While we are aware that appearance is what is important to hypocrites, we always ought to be scrupulous about hygiene, and to dress becomingly with the accent on modesty, and always living within one's means. There is a becomingness linked with the throne, like the apparel of Solomon's servants. A uniform to wear is not in the writer's mind, but the spiritually sensitive man or woman will have an unction about what is becoming in the various circumstances of life.

Pharaoh's dreams and their content are told: the far-reaching interpretation will affect the known world. Notice how -

Joseph's dreams have a personal and family destiny;
the butler and baker's dreams have eternal destiny;
Pharaoh's dreams have world-wide repercussions.

The interpretations tell of a seven-year calamity. The

second seven years tell of barrenness, poverty and misery. He tells the King of the calamity but also offers the remedy. He does not suggest or propose, he speaks with authority.

While all these interpretations and wise counsels are given, it has all been prefaced with an outstanding modesty. He has given God credit and reminds the king of God's supremacy in all matters concerning the nations. The king has no idea that God has in mind the small nondescript group in Canaan, Jacob and his family. God has a destined purpose for Israel and He will exalt whom He will and displace as quickly those who will thwart His divine decrees.

The remedy for Egypt's ills is a man, a man to superintend, to administrate, to gather, to dispense, to distribute wisely, to build, to store, to save much people alive. The story of Joseph's rise to glory is something breathtaking, unbelievable by any human standard. One day in the prison forlorn, forgotten (but not by God), where patience has perfected her work; and now the reward, clothed suitably for his station, the ring of Pharaoh on his hand. Now he is invested with authority, and finally the command from the throne is "Bow the knee" (Gen 41:43). Here is the beginning of the nations bowing to Joseph. How strange and prophetic to see the Gentiles bow to him before his own people do. What a glorious period these seven years were when the Gentile world acknowledged Joseph's greatness. He now wears the linen coat (v.42). This is the first mention of such a garment. Priests and Levites and even David (in priestly joy wearing a linen ephod) shall wear it. What a lovely sight to see the martyred priests of Nob dying in their linen garments. May we like Joseph be distinguished by our linen garment; like David, be zealous and dance in the linen garment; and like the faithful priests, die in our linen garment.

Not only is he publicly acknowledged but also he is given a bride. This so beautifully compensates the rejection he has formerly known. His new name is very apt and precious, Zaphnathpaaneah (the Revealer of Secrets or the Saviour of the World). What a lovely picture of our Lord Jesus as the Revealer of Secrets, "In whom are hid all the treasures of wisdom and knowledge" (Col 2:3); and as the Saviour of the World, "He hath done all things well" (Mark 7:37). The facts of the dream came to pass and the plenty was realised, and the administration was in the hand of Joseph.

CHAPTER 5

Joseph the Governor

(Gen 42 - 45)

How pleasant it is to the righteous mind to see good overcoming evil. Joseph had been hated, traded, slandered, forgotten, and one would almost feel that his best years had passed him by. Also in Egypt he had been subjected to abuse, seduction and neglect. But for the post he was to occupy he needed all these years in the school of God. Leadership is so important to God that when Paul legislates for elders he is quite terse in his language, "not a novice" (1 Tim 3:6), firstly for his own sake lest he be bloated with importance and thus fall into the same condemnation as the devil; secondly, for the people's sake. How moving to hear Israel say of David, "Thou wast he that leddest out and broughtest in Israel" (1 Chron 11:2). What he had learned with sheep on the Judean hills around Bethlehem he continued in the sphere of leadership among the Lord's people.

This final coat, the linen garment given to Joseph (Gen 41:42), is the fourth coat he wears. How remarkable to see all these patriarchs moving to one end yet all different in personality and experience: Abraham's four altars, Isaac's four wells, Jacob's four pillars, and Joseph's four coats. We see also that Joseph is faithful in every house he enters: his father Jacob's, Potiphar's, Pharaoh's, and eventually his own in the rearing of his two children. One can think of the four seasons of our christian experience; the spring, summer, autumn and winter. It is helpful to see Paul as a well-seasoned man, he was with the saints "at all seasons" (Acts 20:18).

51

Joseph saw fruitfulness in his home. Two sons are born to him before the famine came. First was Manasseh, "God hath made me forget all my toil and all my father's house" (Gen 41:51). He has been enabled to forget all that was done to him before, and all the hardship he had been brought into. How precious when the peaceable fruits of righteousness are brought forth. Then came Ephraim, "God hath caused me to be fruitful in the land of my affliction" (Gen 41:52). Here was Joseph placed in this alien land, away from every holy influence, yet he traces the blessing of God in his experience.

Corn in Egypt

Joseph is now installed as the second in the land, riding in the second chariot, exalted by Pharaoh, respected by all. We see in Joseph some of his father's early training put into practice. He went out through all the land, he had and needed officers, but he did not delegate what was his responsibility. He was not only governor in name, he was seen to govern. What he had foretold came to pass; the grain of Egypt came by handfuls. In this section we see Joseph's wisdom in the affairs of earth. Knowing the future he makes preparation. In the light of dispensational truth are we as active to store up? We have been warned that in coming days, things shall wax worse and worse. Are we storing up the rich spiritual bounty of God? We should value greatly all the spiritual enrichment brought to us by those who buy the truth, but this passage so clearly exhibits that God is working all things after the counsel of His own will. Egypt shall be blessed but it shall be for Israel's sake. God intends this nation to give asylum to Jacob's posterity. Generations still unborn shall at first be sheltered here and finally suffer under a rigorous regime. Oh, to grasp clearly that God has a purpose, and we must emphasise that the only way to happiness is to find out the part which God desires us to share in it. Such was the fruit of the land; it was likened to the sand of the sea, "very much" (Gen 41:49). Oh, to be in the field or city where God will bless; no stint, no meanness with Him. The corn was in "handfuls" (v.47), then like "sand of the sea" (v.49). Very much later God will send more blessing on Israel. In the wilderness he rained down manna, the water gushed out of the rock and ran down. To grasp the bountiful character of God is to deliver one's self from a fearful way of living, for fear is the antithesis of faith.

The seven years of plenty are now ended. Egypt has now become the world's granary. All the adjacent lands feel the pinch of poverty and the family of Jacob is not exempted. In fact, all these things have come about for their recovery, discipline and preservation. But in the land of Egypt there was bread.

The acknowledgement of Joseph was the salvation of Egypt; the rejection of Joseph was the reason for the penury of the people of God. All blessing is dependent on where we place Joseph - in the pit, or on the throne. Notice I offer no middle ground, for if Christ be not Lord of all He will not be Lord at all. Is there a department of our lives Christ has not access to? Is there a dark recess His light has not shone into? Is there a truth we have avoided or excused ourselves from acknowledging? Thus it follows we have miserable experiences and we have power neither with God nor man.

The advice of Pharaoh to the Egyptians was first to bow to Joseph, acknowledge his true worth; and then go to Joseph, acknowledge his wisdom, and share in the bounty of his great provision. Not only "go unto Joseph", but also "what he saith to you, do". Here we feel we are in the New Testament and with the Lord at the wedding in Cana of Galilee. Mary His mother said to the servants, "Whatsoever He saith unto you, do it" (John 2:5). Here is something beyond mere acknowledgement, it is obedience, the secret of further joy. "If any man will do His will, he shall know of the doctrine, whether it be of God" (John 7:17). Herein is the reason for many a promising christian life. In the flush of first love and relief from our burden of sin, we made evident progress. Then we found that God had not only spoken about heaven and hell, the world and the devil, but He had also given the last word on every subject, matters of doctrine, dispensations, matrimony, employment and ethics. What matters most is not the grasping with the mind the doctrines of the Bible, but the transferring of them into practice: "as the truth is in Jesus" (Eph 4:21). Paul says, "Thou hast fully known my doctrine, manner of life" (2 Tim 3:10). We shall continue to experience fruitless and powerless preaching unless we fix our hearts on the great pattern, the One who "began to do and teach" (Acts 1:1).

Joseph opened the storehouses. The mercy which these storehouses contained could not be calculated, and thanksgiving is due to him who so provided. On a lesser scale I view the ministry of the Word of God in this respect. These storehouses were the result of Joseph's toils and diligence to see them full for the time ahead. It is a spiritual and proper thing to acknowledge those who instead of hobbies and leisure and even legitimate matters, have given themselves to provide bread for God's people. It is to be noticed that Joseph did not give away the corn for nothing, the people had "to buy". A reason why truth is lightly esteemed is because it was never bought. Someone has said the scourge of our day is men preaching about things they have never felt, and possibly truth that has cost them nothing. It is with honour we revere the memory of those who not only separated from unscriptural institutions but their wives and families felt the pinch and paid the price for the convictions held. Two of such men the writer can recall with vividness are Mr M Grant and Mr E Grant, the former writing the much loved pamphlet 'Twice Delivered'. They left their pulpit and stipend and comfortable surroundings to move by faith. The reverence, humility and dignity of these men have left lasting impressions on the land. The price of this bread may not be as great as it has been to others, but time and prayer and motive-searching is the price to be paid to have bread available for the children of God.

Joseph is probably thirty-seven or thirty-eight years of age at this time. Twenty years have run their course. He himself has known changes, but so also have his father and his brethren. Twenty years ought to make a vast change as the outward man is perishing and the inward man is growing day by day. How exact are God's dealings with us all, especially with families. Corn was the first subject of Joseph's dreams, now corn is the subject again. They had said, "We shall see what will become of his dreams" (Gen 37:20). Imperceptibly and unerringly God's purpose will come to pass. He will move, uproot, cause to journey, but His word shall come to pass. Let none think they will outwit God. "Whom ye slew and hanged on a tree, Him hath God exalted" (Acts 5:30,31). God will bring to ruin every scheme and plan which has not his divine signature. Let "the heathen rage", let "the people imagine a vain thing", but God has said His King will "sit upon My holy hill of Zion" (Psalm 2:6).

It is Jacob, Joseph's father who hears there is corn in Egypt. Possibly the famine is felt most by this fatherly figure who still feels the responsibility, though his sons by now must be between fifty and sixty years of age. He is conscious that this is heaven-sent, he knows that God withholds blessing with something in view. God wants us to be exercised about these national matters like famine, plagues and moral diseases. His word to his sons is, "Get you down" (Gen 42:2). Here begins the process of going down, coming down, and bowing down. Little did they know what this journey would entail. If men will not bow down to the revealed truth of God, God has got time, He waits long, but it is inevitable they shall be exposed and humiliated, and Joseph honoured and exalted. The advice is "buy for us", corn has to be purchased; now a price has to be paid for their failure to submit. Having used much time and energy, and in strange surroundings, a sense of uneasiness marks these men. Sin in differing degrees affects them, old age does not blot out the memory of deceit and lies and crookedness. None of them is young, and now they are uprooted, away from home, and dependent on the charity of others for their existence. These things do not sit well on undisciplined souls; but so different with Joseph.

The brothers' coming to Egypt

The great moment of meeting is most remarkable. As they arrive, Joseph is there; he could have been anywhere in the land of Egypt but God destines these moments and weaves them into His eternal counsel. Twenty years have passed and Joseph's eyes and memory will never forget. How sad their blindness is; he knows and they know not. The most heart-rending fact of the New Testament is "He was in the world, and the world was made by Him, and the world knew Him not. He came unto His own, and His own received Him not" (John 1:10,11). He even pitched his tent alongside ours (became a neighbour to us). I have found the greatest damage to communion with Christ is our wilful blindness. It is the characteristic of Eli the priest, Samson the judge, Johoiachin the king, Israel the nation, and Laodicea the church. No wonder eye salve is recommended so that we might view things from God's standpoint or from His side of the altar.

Here we have a departure from Joseph's normal attitude; he speaks roughly to them. This was not the general tenor of Joseph's make-up. He must have been respectful to his father, he certainly was transparent with his brothers when he revealed to them his dreams, and his courteous disposition won him a steward's position. We note also his modesty in language with his seductress, and his cheerfulness in the prison. This attitude of offhandedness with his brothers was to discover their attitudes and to get from them what he wanted to know most. The accusation, "Ye are spies," was what they thought he was doing for their father at home when he brought "their evil report" (Gen 37:2). They counter this accusation by saying, "We be true men." What Joseph thought of this claim will not be any surprise to any of us, yet a lesson from this is unavoidable. What claims people make, especially when in a difficult situation! When men are truly honest they will not need to advertise that goodness. Generally a man's face and eyes are a good indication of his heart; words are easily spoken. When Ahithophel spoke it was as if he inquired at the oracle of God, but his words "were smoother than butter, softer than oil" (Psalm 55:21), but treachery was in his heart.

I would like to raise a warning on this matter. Nowadays I hear the saints saying, "He is a good speaker," or they say, "He has ability." Few enquire, "Is he a good man, is he an honest employee, is he a loving husband, respected by his wife, is he a generous father, is he devoted to christian interests locally?" How can any brother find satisfaction in christian service who is not first true to God, to his family and to his fellow saints? Joseph's questions have found out his family's fortunes. His father is still alive, his brother Benjamin is at home, no risks have been taken by Jacob.

The probing of Joseph into his brethren's truthfulness is most direct: "Ye are spies," If there be truth in them, he will get to the root of the matters in their lives. They expostulate and tell of the twelve sons born to one man, the youngest is at home, the other is not. Actually whilst one was at home, the other was in their presence. He highlights his distrust by putting them three days in prison "all together into ward" (Gen 42:17). Imagine these ten men in close confinement, only a little taste of the 'medicine' Joseph had for more than ten years.

They will be freed only if they bring Benjamin, Joseph's full blood brother, when they return. This is the turning point of the history of this family, "And they said one to another, we are verily guilty concerning our brother, in that we saw the anguish of his soul, when he besought us, and we would not hear" (Gen 42:21). Herein lies the secret of their recovery, though not yet effected. They would not hear his cries, hear his word, and hear his purpose; they would hear it soon.

57

Reuben speaks up to remind them that he had pleaded and emphasised that he was only a child "but ye would not hear". The secret of our progress is in the hearing what God says to us.

Simeon is taken and bound before their eyes, and shall be guarantee against their return. It has been often wondered why Simeon was chosen. Was it possibly because he was the most forward in his hatred of Joseph? He has given ample evidence already of cruel elements in his make up, and now he is given time to think well of his past deeds, not only at Dothan but at Shechem, where he and Levi are marked by gross barbarity, and thus has begun the great recovery of this elected family. God is sitting over its affairs as the refiner, and He will apply the fire where necessary. He will bring His own purpose to pass and longs for His likeness to be reflected in the gold being refined.

He fills the sacks. This is so characteristic of Joseph - not speaking roughly but giving - magnanimously. Here too is the heart of Christ. He will find a multitude whose only motive was loaves and fishes. They in turn would make him King, but only on economic grounds. In that way shall Israel fall foul of the antichrist, for when they are without a friendly nation he shall provide an economic miracle for them. Thus the base nature of the nation as pictured in Judas shall again raise its head till it finds the antichrist sitting as god in the Temple, the money in sacks. Whatever God bestows upon His people, whether in Old or New Testament, it is always at His cost. Every christian grace and virtue are all at His expense and are freely dispensed by Him. When they sold Joseph they said, "What profit?" He says, "Fill the sacks," well shaken, running over, not taking but rather returning their money.

Here Joseph is teaching an indirect lesson. He knows them and what they think and talk about, yet he worked with them. He knew the drift of their lives, they would never have given the money back, they would have 'cashed in' and upped the price, and taken the best advantage of the market's instability. How humbling to meet a soul who has found the secret of living, in giving, like Joseph here, to the most unworthy and the least deserving.

They are on their journey a little way when one needed to feed his ass. The money is discovered! Here they are in a strange situation, they have money they would rather be without! How strange are the ways of God, to bring us to hate the things we loved and felt could not live without. It is at this point we see another step in their recovery. "What is this that God has done unto us?" (Gen 42:28). This is the first record of these men's God-consciousness. They know and feel God is near, yet they feel awkward. Unconfessed sin is the greatest disadvantage to the child of God.

Sin is not weakness, sin is wickedness, and it makes us uneasy and uncomfortable in the presence of purity. An offering was available in Israel for sins of ignorance. Note these were not glossed over, whether in the ordinary Israelite or the most separated Nazarite who could not touch a dead body; whether in a disobedient prophet though he is old, whether in Eli the priest's sons, or Samuel the prophet's sons, or in David the king's sons. Sins of ignorance are followed by David's secret sins, those things that are practised but not before human eyes, yet before the Almighty. What folly it is for us to care or fear man more than God. But God's Word speaks also of presumptuous sins. These, in the writer's judgement, are the most serious because we presume to know better than God. Passages of inspired Scripture are spoken of as if they are optional or additional things, and in many quarters when matters of practice and ethics are raised, some feel it is open to opinion. Upon this point shall hang possibly even our eternal destiny. If we receive the Word of God then we must receive it as the truth of God. I find it difficult to accept that God was waiting for this or any other generation to add, subtract or better His revelation. No one sound in faith would even attempt to deny the great fundamental truths of Scripture, but the height or depth of a man's spirituality is to bow before every spoken word of the Lord. Every brother must realise that the Scripture teaches that he should function publicly in the assembly (I do not mean only by preaching). Every sister should see clearly scriptural injunctions to silence in church gatherings. Paul is clear that men's hair ought to be short, or else it is shameful; and God says the woman's hair is her creatorial glory, it is for her enhancement. Matters of business associations are so clearly spoken of: "Be ye not unequally yoked together with unbelievers" (2 Cor 6:14). Matters of dress are clearly taught and everywhere modesty is encouraged. So too are attitudes to parents, attitudes to politics, attitudes to our progeny, attitudes to our employer. Why I have raised these matters is because in these brothers of Joseph, their sins were in realms of the family, domestic and very ordinary. They did not deny the existence of God but they wanted not the rule of God.

The scene on their arrival at home is curious. Most domestic scenes are very ordinary. Certain ones stand out, but God will not hide what He wants to be public. The last scene at home was a blood-covered coat and an ambiguous story; now the sacks of corn are full, and all from the man whom they hated and to whom they could not speak civilly. To their horror they see not only corn but also the money. The sight of the money made them afraid. Had they not sold Joseph for money and now this! The lesson of this twice-repeated finding should not be lost. Jacob and his whole family, for I think they would all be gathered, were to learn that the seeking of material things was what had brought disaster and tragedy to them, and also learn that someone else did not have thoughts like that. I have observed in my many travels when in the presence of Christians who are mean (this is a paradox), how awkward and embarrassed they are when some philanthropic deed is rehearsed, as if the people who do these things are assumed to have plenty;

yet it was out of extreme poverty there abounded the richness of some saints' liberality. Thus not only the heads of this family, but everyone, will witness this beneficence. Jacob finds opportunity to upbraid his sons and he does not hide what has smouldered within him for years, that they were behind the ultimate exodus of Joseph from his home.

The circumstances related to Jacob caused him to face the facts: Joseph is not, and Simeon is not, and now this further possibility of Benjamin being taken from him. With burdened heart he groans, "All these things are against me" (Gen 42:36). What deep depressions gather over the spirit of the most princely of people. Had not Jacob seen the ladder and the angels and the Lord at the top of the ladder? Had God not kept him all his life long, had he not wrestled and won, was he not Israel? No, not here; it is Jacob who says, "All these things are against me." Here is human reasoning. This is not the thinking of Israel. Little did he know that all these things were for him, God would work out the circumstances to bring him where want shall never be known, famine shall never be felt; fear of surrounding tribes shall give place to Goshen with and peace and rest.

In the interval the corn is soon eaten up for the famine was sore. Jacob put away from him the fateful day. He is hard pressed to part with Benjamin, although Reuben has already offered his two sons if anything befalls the lad. This left Jacob unimpressed! How true this lesson is. Those of an unstable character are given little credence, and some of their offers and suggestions are very sensational, "slaying my two sons". In this time the ten sons will have had time to digest their Egypt experience and they too put off the evil day when they must return. Now Jacob has to speak, "Go again, buy us a little food" (Gen 43:2). Judah now comes into the scene again, he who was behind the selling of Joseph. He reminds his father of the futility of returning without Benjamin. Jacob frets and scolds their lack of wisdom in telling all their business, but here in this family quarrel, a quality of character emerges bordering on nobility. Judah says, "Send the lad with me, I will be surety for him" (Gen 43:8,9). Here is a man changed, here is someone who is prepared to take the family burden and the responsibility at his own personal expense; here is a man not putting up his sons, or means, or ability, but he is prepared to be extinct himself forever.

Israel bows to the inevitable, the crushing weight of circumstances and evidences causes him to yield. We see here such a beautiful scene as the father projects his mind right down into Egypt. He will placate the Governor with a present. What he is trying to do, he is saying, we need corn, it is the staff of life, but we are not beggars. He is saying, don't go down empty handed, take the man a present, treat him as a superior, show that you acknowledge these distinctions, honour to whom honour is due; the little balm for wounds, the little honey for sweetness, spices and myrrh for fragrance, nuts and almonds for fruitfulness. Take double money in your hand, prove that you are righteous men. He then accepts the will of God with much reluctance. I would like to draw the lesson from this as to how reluctant we are to fall in with God's plans for us, our own reasoning the greatest barrier to bowing to His will.

Their second coming to Egypt

The scenes at the second coming into Egypt are most moving. Nothing is so sad to behold as a group of guilt-conscious men. When we were first introduced to them they were so bold and arrogant and abrasive; now they are in another land and dependent and needy. Now they are brought low. They have had God resisting them these twenty years: "God resisteth the proud but giveth grace to the humble" (James 4:6). Herein lies the deep malaise behind private and public fruitlessness, and the same principle affects assembly life and many wonder why God has not blessed. It is because He resisteth the proud. Are we proud of our church position, our orthodoxy? Are we proud of the ability granted to us? Hear the great church builder say, "What hast thou that thou didst not receive?" (1 Cor 4:7). Are we proud of third and fourth generations of Christians in our families? That would border on assuming God's continued blessing to us. With what vaunted words have we heard of what assemblies and individuals have done in the gospel, and yet we continue to preach and few have ever been honoured by anyone being truly converted under their preaching. This passage shows us that all the corn and all the money and all the talking never for a moment would have changed these men. It was all preparatory to the moment when Joseph would show himself. If they were self conscious or sin conscious, Joseph was very patient and completely controlled; "Bring these men home" (Gen 43:16). Whatever the day will hold for them all, with joy or judgement, Joseph shall be alone with them. Whatever they did to him, he will not expose their shame, nor add to their discomfort. How beautiful it is not only to do the right thing but do it in a right way. How genuine to see Ebedmelech sending down the pit to Jeremiah the old cast cloths and rotten rags so that he would not feel the discomfort of the ropes on his arms.

The steward of Joseph's house is a great example of his master's influence. He calms them and makes them know that God is behind the scenes. He shows and offers them every courtesy and treats them with great politeness.

The coming of Joseph at noon to his house is very significant. The light is shining in its brilliance, transparency and light and truth are the subject. The light is beginning to dawn on blind eyes, the dark corners of every soul are being searched; nothing can be hid at noon, no mist, no shadows, the burning heat. It is strange how the human heart constantly seeks self-justification: the present, the money, and the brother they had been asked to bring. What things have yet to be revealed by the Sun of Righteousness! While the present was precious in its variety, yet we see them bringing this to find acceptance before Joseph. One tear of true repentance would have been better than all these diplomatic approaches. If only Cain had brought that which spoke of his hatefulness of sin and self, how blessed he would have been, but the seriousness of sin and its consequences had never gripped him. Sin, whether in the sinner or the child of God, is a serious matter. We can only truly know sin forgiven when sin has been forsaken. Such blindness on these men's part is inexcusable. Here are ten men, now increased to eleven with the presence of Benjamin, and not one of them can discern Joseph. His language and dress were different, his age is around forty. With Joseph, all seems in control till he comes face to face with Benjamin, his own blood brother. Here melts the glacier, here roughness vanishes, here his disciplined chemistry falters, he seeks a place to weep. Here all the pent up well springs give place to torrents of tears over twenty years of bottled up sorrow, suffering, anguish, and iron in his soul. Even in his exalted glory he felt utterly lonely without his brethren. Let the true child of God remember that once we have tasted of the gracious purposes of our God no amount of Egyptian glory can eclipse it. Egypt truly valued is nothing compared to the greater treasure of reproach for Christ.

Just a few very ordinary points which ought not to be missed. "Is your father well, the old man of whom ye spake? Is he yet alive?" (Gen 43:27). Joseph will show his concern in a moment to the young man Benjamin, but first to the old man. Would that we in this generation had got our priorities right. What time and labour too is expended to promote our young people, and this is proper in its place; but what a grave mistake, yea injustice, that those who have done, given and left us so much, should be discarded, and when years fail and strength ebbs, are easily discouraged. It is one of the most moving scenes to see the Lord's mother being the subject of His tender care at the cross. Notice who lodged Paul in the Acts, it was an old disciple. Notice who brought beds and basins and help to David in his stressful hour, it was Barzillai, an old man of eighty years of age. Notice the faithful ones at the remembrance in Malachi's day. Notice the remnant in the temple in Luke, Zacharias and Elizabeth, Simeon and Anna. Notice the wisdom of our Lord in John 21, sheep twice to be fed, lambs once. "Is your father well?" Have you requited your parents? If you don't you are worse than an unbeliever. Many a man or woman now would love to have a mother and father to visit and take a present or a parcel to, but while they were living they could not find time from a seemingly busy spiritual schedule to see if their father was well.

The family of Joseph now bows down to him again. They describe themselves as "thy servants". This is a far cry from the well's mouth, the fields and flocks, but God will have the last say. The world has yet to see Scripture fulfilled, for "every knee should bow - and that every tongue should confess that Jesus Christ is Lord, to the glory of God the Father" (Phil 2:10,11). Joseph gives Benjamin a personal blessing, "God be gracious unto thee my son" (Gen 43:29). Benjamin is different; he is free from the guilt of selling Joseph, he has not the duplicity of the others, and an unspoiled purity still exists. The Lord has blessing for such lives. To keep oneself pure is the longing of a spiritual father for his son in the faith (1 Tim 5:22).

Here is recorded one of the scenes of pathos unequalled in the Bible. Joseph made a hasty retreat, for his bowels yearned for his younger brother. He yearned over the lost years of his fellowship and friendship, yearned to think he had to live with such men as his brethren were. What experiences have there been in life when we sought our chamber to weep our salt tears, never knowing that God was collecting them in His bottles. So here are true tears. A bottle will hold a lifetime's once we exclude the crocodile and feigned ones, and the great amount caused by remorse like Esau. The genuine ones God loves and cherishes and values.

After this great scene, Joseph washes and we see his self-control emerging, he refrains himself. Then he sets on bread. One can imagine the wholesomeness of this bread of Joseph's table, full of nourishment. He kept separate because of known customs in Egypt. This was a mark of wisdom. While he acknowledges Egypt's scruples about Hebrews, he also acknowledges the becoming order in the Hebrew home; seventeen when he left home and the honour and order of that home never forgotten. The firstborn, the eldest, were given their place. The youngest accepted their place and did not demur, but when it came to Benjamin he was singled out for particular blessing. Joseph seems to act in a sovereign way, giving what is his own to whom he will. The men marvel that this seeming Egyptian is aware of such intimate detail of order in a Hebrew home.

We now approach the most embarrassing experience of Joseph's family. They are only hours away from discovery, only a brief time and they shall experience perplexity. The night at Joseph's home had closed with merriment and, although in close proximity with Joseph, it never entered their minds who he was. Joseph has yet a final lesson he wants his brethren to learn. He has seen a change in their attitudes, whether wrought by grace or experience one would not know, or just diplomatic servility owing to their dependent position, or were they just getting wiser with age? Sometimes age does to people what grace was not allowed to do. But one more day of pressure shall be brought upon them. Joseph wants reality and a deep repentance, which will never be forgotten for generations.

Joseph instructs his steward, "Fill the sacks with food, as much as they can carry" (Gen 44:1). Here again is further evidence of the philanthropic nature of Joseph. Even when they have not as yet repented, nor as yet adjusted, he is still heaping mercies upon them. How true this has been in life's experience. When we deserved His rod, He loaded us with benefits and broke our hearts with His provisions. The placing of the cup in Benjamin's sack is a matter of great importance. Whether he had a real divining cup or otherwise is not very important. Had he copied the Egyptian diviners? One wonders in Elisha's case how he sent Gehazi with his staff to raise the Shunammite's boy. The result is significant. Joseph wants to see their attitude to his own blood brother Benjamin.

They are not far removed from the city when the steward halts them and states his business. From the happy scenes of being honoured guests of the man who was next to Pharaoh, to this experience by the roadside accused of treachery and at least robbery, they stoutly defend their reputation with some evidence of their honesty. They remind him of the money returned and brought all the way from Canaan. So sure are they of their innocence they swear that whoever has done this shall forfeit his life, and their liberty also is brought into the covenant.

The steward mitigates their offence, saying with whomsoever the cup is found shall be servant and the others blameless. Then began the searching by the steward: from the eldest to the least, showing to us that the possibilities lay latent in them all. Consternation could not describe the scene when the cup was discovered in Benjamin's sack. The implications of this and the gravity of the situation are felt by these men. Here they stand with rent clothes and bowed heads, remonstrating their innocence. Would they think of the day when they rent the clothes off Joseph's back? Now anguish grips them like they have never felt before. They feel they are dealing with powers and influences that they cannot stop. The tangled web of life has surely crept over them. Here they are making for home, asses laden, and food plentiful, anticipating a welcome homecoming. This time they have had great success in the land of Egypt and dined with the man, now this awful reversal of circumstances. What a painful journey back to the city, heads bowed, spirits chastened, speechless in their own defence.

At Joseph's house we see a moving scene rarely repeated

in any literature. Joseph's words ring out to touch heart and conscience, "What deed is this that ye have done?" (Gen 44:15). Did the memory of former days and deeds done enter their mind? The stolen cup is light compared with a life of moral and commercial evil, and the evil they brought on their father. Joseph's reminder, "Did ye not know that such an one as I can certainly divine?" is a jolting of their memory to many other things they had been told but had treated with contempt.

We now enter that section of the story that has all the hallmarks of nobility. Judah speaks on behalf of his brethren; he is the leader and shows why by his great lawyer's plea. This is the first lawyer's plea in the Scriptures. A comparison between Judah and Tertullus in Acts 24 is worth examination. Judah first put the whole eleven under Joseph's bondage but Joseph will have none of it. Judah was he who "sold Joseph". Judah had said, "What profit is it if we slay our brother, and conceal his blood? Come, and let us sell him" (Gen 37:26,27). Here Joseph will see if time and experience has changed Judah. "Then Judah came near" (Gen 44:18). Here is one of the most appealing pleas ever recorded, if not the most. The language is exceptional, the pathos so moving. He speaks of Benjamin as the lad; he speaks of his father with a dignity begotten of deep respect. He tells of his father's heartbreak and great loss, he tells of his grey hairs, he tells of his father's suspicion of the lad going with them, then he tells of his promise to be surety for Benjamin. His appeal culminates in words calculated to touch the heart. He asks to be a bondman in Benjamin's place, he asks to go out of existence as long as Benjamin goes free. Here is the great arrival of Judah's experience. He is prepared to take another's place, to bear another's guilt, to take upon him another's shame. What a thought that He who sprang out of Judah would come and take our place, bear our shame and die on account of sin not His own.

The final plea in his supplication to Joseph is so poignant:

"How shall I go up to my father, and the lad be not with me" (v.34). Here then was what Joseph had longed for, that Judah, so representing the nation and leadership, had come to think of the future generation seen in Benjamin, and would have great depths of feeling for the past generation seen in his father Israel.

Joseph made known in Egypt

Chapter 45 opens with the telling word "then". Whenever we read "then", we should say "when?" When such repentance and heart-rending pleas for others are made, when self and self-interests are lost sight of and only the good and wellbeing of others are pleaded, Joseph is broken down. Joseph in chapter 45 is now at the age of thirty-nine. He has heard Judah's plea for Benjamin and he must have been moved by Judah's growing concern for his elderly father. Spiritual progress comes from a base of repentance, and grows to a deep compassionate concern for both old and young. Judah is growing in holiness, for he is growing in kindness. This most delicate of meetings has a great dispensational context. Here is Joseph about to reveal himself to his brethren. The day when the nation of Israel discovers the value, the worth, the honour and glory of the Messiah whom they rejected, set at naught, and disallowed, they shall be "troubled at His presence" (v.3).

What great matters now unfold. "Cause every man to go out from me" (Gen 45:1). Here is a scene that Joseph will not allow even one Egyptian eye to see. "And there stood no man with him, while Joseph made himself known unto his brethren." While Joseph made himself known unto his brethren, and serious matters were about to be enacted, blame apportioned, and tears to be wept, there must be no prying eyes. This is the family of faith, though up to this time they have shown little evidence of it. Joseph rehearses all that has happened since he saw them at the well's mouth in the desert at Dothan. He does not hide the fact that they sold him. There is brought before them now the culmination of their contempt and envy. But far and beyond their grievous deed, how did they feel when he said, "I am Joseph"? - Joseph of the dreams, Joseph of the disclosures, Joseph of the coat of many colours. What a moment for them then, what a moment for us all when He shall say, "I am Jesus." Will we stand like these men mute? Have we not a past? Self-seeking is a displacing of Christ. Envy is a matter that must reap a harvest. Embarrassment awaits all that will not have Joseph in his God-appointed place. Silence is yet the portion of all who have treated God's truth with derision. Oh that the Scriptures would awaken us to the fact that God reveals His truth to be obeyed, not speculated upon, or treated as an optional extra.

Joseph has been twenty-two years away from home, and in his address to his brothers the name of God and God's purpose are linked with every experience in those years. He talks of the past, "whom ye sold" (v.4). He talks of the present, "God made me a father to Pharaoh" (v.8). He talks of the future. We see here a portrayal of Him who was, who is, and who is to come. How skilfully he mitigates all that was done to him. "Be not grieved or angry with yourselves" (v.5). How magnanimous is Joseph. He finds it nothing to forgive when grief is in evidence.

I have often tried to enter into these men's thoughts, especially when Joseph opened to them the future. Five more years of famine to go, starvation and death to stare them in the face, but Joseph has a future for them. Wherever sin is grieved over and repented of, there is a future. The moment Peter wept bitterly, the moment of recovery had begun. One feels this point must be stressed. Along the road to heaven many wrecks lie, firstly because they never grasped the serious nature of sin. Even useful and fruitful servants of the Lord, whether overseers or deacons, who have made shipwreck in a moral and doctrinal way, have, in seeking to come back into public preaching, forgotten the clear injunction of Paul, that any public service must only be carried on by blameless men.

The moving scenes in the chapter reveal his tears, his heart longings for fellowship, his pent up feelings for his blood-brother Benjamin. He weeps at his neck, and then he kisses them all. Nothing but love and grace flow from a heart that God has chastened. This is the moment that produces the fruit of all the suffering and loneliness, and the experience of the "iron in his soul". Only after that did his brethren talk with him.

The Egyptians were overjoyed to see Joseph so happy. They knew his value but they were also conscious that Joseph was lonely and would not fit into Egyptian ways, so to be able to accommodate his family pleased them well. The good of the land is promised. Goshen is fertile, large and plentiful. Joseph gives out changes of raiment to all his brethren. They are fitted out suitably to him who was on the throne of the land of Egypt. To Benjamin he bestows wealth, three hundred pieces of silver and five changes of raiment. How blessed it is to know that although we have failed and have been carnal, though not excusing it, yet we shall be clothed suitable to our relationship with Him. Yet for those who have not defiled their garment and those who have overcome, white raiment and great glory shall be bestowed (Rev 3:4). How shallow our minds if we imagine that Demas and Paul are going to be equal in glory, that Lot and Abraham shall be viewed alike. Heaven will assess the quality of our character, our contribution, and the purity of our motives. Every one of them received a garment, but Benjamin five garments and three hundred pieces of silver.

The abundance sent to his father is more than moving, ten asses laden with good things, "bread and corn and meat for the way". Was this in answer to Jacob's present to the man, a little honey and a little balm and the best fruits of the land? Here we see Joseph doing things after a godly sort, which is a manner worthy of God. This matter is deeper than just general kindness to his parent. Jacob could have managed to Egypt on much less but Joseph's mind is not like the many. He knows the God that sends the corn by handfuls, and anyway this corn was for this family's preservation. When Jesse, David's father, sent him with provisions for his brothers he sent a cheese for their captain as well. We might say he would have enough, but these mean calculations never entered Jesse's mind. Many meetings are small because those who lead them have small minds and hearts as to the work of God. As he sent his brothers home to bring their families he warns them, "See that ye fall not out by the way" (v.24). I have always thought what he meant was, "Don't begin to blame one another or apportion blame now". His insight into human nature was most remarkable. He does not want them losing out in the purpose of God at this stage. That no incident occurred was very precious and we are sure most pleasant.

The return to their father is again a poignant scene. None can enter a father's heart like a father: all the male children gone, all the weight of the family resting on him, no swift communications, just day after day with no news. It is good for the new generation to understand the feelings of parents. They have begotten you and in childhood nursed and loved you. Only rarely do we find, even in christian circles a requiting of parents. Requiting may not be in the monetary sense of Scripture, but at least it ought to be in respect and honour and obedience.

Joseph is yet alive. Jacob had thought for twenty-two years that he was dead, but still more startling, "He is Governor over all the land of Egypt". "Jacob's heart fainted" (v.26). The news was astounding, too much for this lonely tired saint. He felt it was another deception they would force upon him, he still will not trust them.

Thinking of our Lord Jesus in relation to this passage, what a moment when the nation hears, "He is alive!" Everything was done to prove that He did not rise from the dead: seal, soldiers, stones, bribes, words put into mouth, "say His disciples stole His body". But He is alive; witness an empty tomb, orderly grave clothes, stone rolled away, appearances in the morning for breakfast on the shore, midday in the upper room for a meal, supper in some ordinary cottage in Emmaus. He was

    seen of Cephas as to the circumcision;
    seen of James as to the local church;
    seen of Paul as to the body of Christ;
    seen of the twelve as to the complete nations;
    seen of above five hundred at once;
    - many infallible proofs.

"Joseph is yet alive, and he is Governor over all the land of Egypt." All the resources are under his governership. Because our heavenly Joseph lives and reigns we shall live and reign, and all the stores and treasures are ours because we are His. We have been the subjects of divine election, the objects of sovereign grace; now we are partakers of the divine nature, children by faith, sonship in resemblance and responsibility, heirs and joint heirs with Christ. How comforting to know our Joseph is Governor of all the land.

When Jacob saw the wagons which Joseph has sent for him "the spirit of Jacob their father revived". He had heard all that Joseph had said, but when he saw the wagons, here was proof beyond doubt; these were for his conveyance. In what grand style Joseph does everything. He thinks of his father's age, he thinks of his necessities, food for the journey; he thinks of his comfort, wagons to carry him. Little wonder the spirit of Jacob revived. When in our calm moments we reflect on all the way the Lord our God has led us we must confess that God's care for our every need has caused us to be revived. If daily we could only recount our former mercies, in them we would find strength and confidence that the God we have trusted for our eternity will surely not leave us now.

And Israel said, "It is enough." (v.28). Here it is no longer

Jacob fainting, or Jacob revived, but Israel accepting; accepting that all his anguish and pain and loneliness were for this moment; that what he had longed for in relation to Joseph had come to pass: but only on the suffering side of life is this brought about. Jacob said, "It is great" (Newberry margin). Oh that our mouths would cry, "It is great": what God hath wrought is great, what Christ has accomplished is great, the purpose of God is great, the chastisement of God is great. The bitter waters have made Elim pleasant. He grasped with William Cowper, the poet and hymn writer,

> *His purposes will ripen fast*
> *Unfolding every hour*
> *The bud may have a bitter taste*
> *But sweet will be the flower.*

What journeys can be taken, distances covered, things overcome, once we have been revived. This was only through the ministry of Joseph; the provision, the laden asses, corn and bread, the wagons, the clothes, and the silver. Jacob was now determined to see the purpose of God wrought out, it was all centred in Joseph.

CHAPTER 6

Joseph the Administrator

(Gen 46 - 50)

"Israel took his journey" (Gen 46:1). Whenever he bows to God's will and revelation he makes progress. For at least twenty-two years, possibly much more, he had no revelation from God; now he wants to sacrifice. After he sacrifices God gives him revelation. God also quietens his fears: "Fear not to go." He gives him promise of a great nation in the future, and of personal joy, "Joseph shall put his hand upon thine eyes" (v.4). God has not only great things in store for the future, but blessing and creature comforts in the present. There follows a genealogy of the children of Israel in its limited sense - seventy souls, they are all going to be blessed.

The meeting between Joseph and Jacob must stand beside other great meetings, like David and Jonathan, Christ and John the Baptist, Paul and Peter. Judah is sent as ambassador to Joseph. What a change has come over this man. "Joseph made ready his chariot" (v.29). The last time he saw his father was in the vale of Hebron. What scenes had passed over him, cruelly stripped and sold, carried as a slave to Egypt, sold in open auction, tempted by its mistress and slandered, put unjustly into prison till the word of the Lord tried him. Now he is in a chariot with attendants, the king's favour shines on him, the world is indebted to him. Let none wilt under the rod of God's providence. God will bring forward whom He will and will depose after His own will.

The meeting of Joseph and his father

These two were the greatest sufferers in the history that we

75

have traced. Those of a spiritual mind feel it when they are parted; no loneliness is so acute as those who see things from God's side of the altar. Joseph was an enigma to his brothers. Jacob would be like someone out of a lost generation to his sons, but Joseph and Jacob understood each other. How strange the atmosphere when spiritual people discuss spiritual things in the company of others, not necessarily unbelievers, who feel they cannot enter into these things. How sad when Martha chides Mary for sitting at His feet while all the time it is she who has need to get her priorities right. Joseph's love for his father is quite akin to his love of Benjamin. Jacob by this time is old and grey-haired and obviously feeble, but Joseph loves him, values him, weeps over him, yea weeps for the years of lost love.

Jacob's first words to his best loved, long lost son are, "Let me die" (v.30). He feels that since he has now seen Joseph nothing else in life matters; and nothing else does matter, and nothing else is more important than having seen Christ. Simeon in the temple longs to get away to another temple not made with hands. He wants to breathe in the air of another clime, he finds the world a colourless place since he had seen the Lord's Christ. Paul's intimate life with Christ made him desire "to be with Christ; which is far better" (Phil 1:23). The goods of Sodom are worthless once you have met the King of Salem. What are things, but for giving away the tithes to Melchisedec, once we have lifted up our hand to the possessor of heaven and earth.

Israel and his sons' introduction to Egypt

Here we see Joseph advising his brethren on their approach to Egypt and Pharaoh. Certain customs are necessary to know; for example, cattle are sacred, sheep abhorred. He entreated his brethren just to tell Pharaoh what they had been from their youth. Joseph knows that possibly no family was so astute in husbandry as his brothers. It must have been pleasant to Joseph to see his five brethren, for he did not bring them all, taking the supplicant's place and impressing the king as they sought his favour. Pharaoh bestows that favour through the medium of

Joseph, also commanding that any showing activity should be placed over the royal herd.

The greater is blessed of the lesser. Here is a picture most marvellous: Joseph the Governor introducing his father to royalty. It must be noticed that he was not ashamed of his elderly parent. It is further noticed that this parent was crippled. He was confident his father would do him honour. What an unexpected outcome: Pharaoh seems quite awkward in his presence. Pharaoh was possibly quite young, for Joseph claimed to be a "father unto Pharaoh". Here is a mighty potentate, ruler of the greatest power in the known world, and all he can ask this old man is, "How old art thou?" (Gen 47:8). He calls his years days; he knows their brevity; he calls them few and evil. He has known much sorrow. He calls his life a pilgrimage. A pilgrim is one who has a future destination. He does not go into every detail before this mighty man. He is concise, he is clear, he is confident, he knows who he is, he knows his age, one hundred and thirty years, he knows life's problems, he knows he has something to give. This mighty father of Joseph is not awed and not arrogant; he blesses Pharaoh. If we contrasted the possessions of each, this would seem the height of presumption. But Pharaoh does not feel that, he feels he is in the presence of another power, and possibly not for the first time, for had he not dealings with God by dreams? If only we all could understand that we have something to impart even to the earth's greatest.

We have thought of Joseph's rise to fame, but what of his father? If we could but have seen him limp over the brook Jabbok, leaning heavily on his staff and on his God, no one would have forecast he would be received at Egypt's court and have an audience with its king. Let us labour the point till it hurts us, that we have something that all around us need. We do not need their blessing, but they do need ours. Only when we have been in touch with God shall we have blessings to impart to others, even kings. Goshen is made over to Israel for Joseph's sake. All blessing that shall come to Israel shall be on the basis of what Christ has done. The future affairs are all centred around Joseph. He nourishes his brethren in Goshen, no harm or want or alarm shall come near them.

From this point onward we see Joseph in a different form. We have seen him as a prophet to his family, rejected, as a slave to Potiphar, as a servant to butler and baker, as a revealer of secrets to Pharaoh, as the nourisher of his brethren in Goshen; but now that the famine increases, we see his administrative abilities come out. In chapter 47 money matters are under his control, financial matters are under his sway. Cattle matters, all the livestock are under his rule; then all the land, then all the people are mortgaged to Pharaoh so that all matters small and great are brought under him; yet his wisdom and compassion are seen in the distribution and retention. Note that even the little ones are on the mind of Joseph. Such wisdom brings from the nation a grateful response.

Under Joseph's benign rule the young nation of Israel prospered, grew and multiplied exceedingly. Joseph would be about fifty-six by the time that Jacob came to die. Seventeen years with Joseph had given him peace and rest he never had all his lifetime. Old age has its own difficulties but here we see a man grow old graciously. If we could keep near to our Joseph we too would keep our souls warm in the things of God.

A death bed scene

How moving was that scene when Joseph met Jacob after so many years, and we are confident they both would have loved it to go on and on, but on earth partings are inevitable. Abraham has to part with Sarah, Isaac with Rebecca, Jacob with Rachael, and we with our loved ones. How sweet the parting when there had been more than physical togetherness, when there had been a spiritual togetherness. Note that in chapter 47 Joseph has a private audience with his father. He will see and speak to all his sons in chapter 49, but he entrusts privately to Joseph matters that are very sacred in relation to his burial and where his bones will lie. While Jacob has valued God's provision in Egypt he knows that all God's purposes for Israel are linked with Canaan. Let everyone who has been blessed of God and favoured, keep before them that:

> *"This is not our place of resting,*
> *Ours a city yet to come;*
> *Onward to it we are hastening,*
> *On to our eternal home.*
>
> *In it all is light and glory,*
> *O'er it shines a nightless day;*
> *Every trace of sin's sad story,*
> *All the curse has passed away."*

At the death bed, all the past comes before Joseph's father, Jacob. He remembers when God revealed Himself at Luz in the land of Canaan. He recalls the blessing, "and blessed me" (Gen 48:3). He remembers vividly the promise, "I will make thee fruitful" (v.4). He tells his son the extent of the promise, "an everlasting possession" (v.4). He encourages Joseph that his two sons, Ephraim and Manasseh, shall not lose out because they were born in Egypt, "are mine" (v.5). He recalls the death of his first and best love, Rachael, "died by me" (v.7).

The incident of Jacob's dimness of vision and his crossing of the hands, seem to alarm Joseph, but not so his father. Success and prosperity had momentarily blunted Joseph's spiritual sensitivity. Jacob will teach him that God always has the second man in His divine purpose. He has something for Joseph's "lads" (v.16), but he has something unique for Joseph, one portion above his brethren. It is a portion that is linked with affliction, "I took out of the hand of the Amorite with my sword and with my bow" (v.22). This portion is given because, out of all the Patriarch's sons, no one ever suffered like Joseph; he was in God's purpose but that involved discipline, suffering, envy, slander, the iron in his soul and his feet hurt with fetters. The double portion is linked with his sorrow; but here is the exceeding and eternal weight of glory. Oh, to call our present state "our light affliction" (2 Cor 4:17).

The family assessor

What a family record is left in chapter 49. Ours is to see Joseph's portion in it, but here is a family viewed through the eyes of their father. When life is near its end we come to value things and people in another light. We will get a leader's estimate of them from Moses later on, and a king's estimate from David; in the home, Jacob; in the wilderness, Moses; and in the land, David.

Joseph beholding his father's death bed must have been moved greatly; firstly to see him finish his course so well with joy, and then to hear from his mouth blessings and spiritual endowments, his unerring judgements on his sons behaviour and their life's motives; and to hear his father's commentary on his own experience. "Joseph is a fruitful bough", not just growth and buds and leaves, but fruit by a well, nourished and kept full of sap by an upspringing source, whose branches run over the wall. Such is the force of this branch it reaches out to others who least expected and not even deserved it.

"The archers have sorely grieved him and shot at him" (Gen 49:23). When he was young and so defenceless, his brothers hated him. But he rose from amidst it all and knew the strength of "the mighty God of Jacob" (v.24). Verse 25 is possibly the greatest source of uplift in Joseph's life, and in any man's life: "even by the God of thy father, who shall help thee".

Notice the width of these blessings. Five times the thought of blessing is mentioned:

shall bless thee -   personal blessing;
(If this is not secured none of the others will be realised.)
blessings of heaven -   spiritual and eternal;
blessing of the deep -   earthly blessing;
blessing of breast and womb -family blessing;
blessing of thy father -   parental blessing.

Jacob had more to leave than his progenitors: bounds of the everlasting hills, boundless blessing. These indescribable blessings are on the head of Joseph and on the crown of the head of him who was separate (or Nazarite) from his brethren. How sad to see how limp these other brothers were in comparison with Joseph.

Chapter 49 continues into chapter 50, describing the beautiful exodus of Jacob; "By faith Jacob, when he was a dying, blessed both the sons of Joseph; and worshipped, leaning upon the top of his staff" (Heb 11: 21). Blessing, leaning, worshipping: God possibly got Jacob to do at the end of life what he would not do during his life, just to lean.

Joseph at the age of fifty-six weeps upon his father's face. Who can evaluate the emotions of Joseph, not just at the passing of a father, but the passing of an epoch? He embalms Israel. That which is of God shall never come to corruption. Oh, that we could learn that nothing of Jacob shall go over into Canaan; only what God has made us shall be preserved. Joseph is at pains to fulfil his father's desires.

Jacob's burial

Joseph went up to bury his father. We can see clearly that Joseph has assumed the firstborn's place. He is now the recognised head of the family, he is over all Egypt and possibly all surrounding nations were tributary to Egypt. His impeccable manners have never left him; he requests leave of the king. How beautiful to see that when we learn submission and sorrow in youth it is a good ally in mature years. What must the nations have thought of this concourse "a very great company" (Gen 50:9). It has been my wonder to behold the burial of many men, and the world wonders why so many gather to pay respect to their neighbour. Hundreds have gathered at some of the humblest men's burials. Joseph will see to it that his father will be honoured, and his will obeyed as to where he will be interred.

Joseph returns with his brethren to Egypt. His brethren begin to feel uneasy. A sad conscience can never be at ease. They thought Joseph would now requite them for their cruelty. In this scene of Joseph with his brethren, this final experience but one, here is Joseph again encouraging his brethren, dispelling their fears, showing to them the purpose of God. He points out that he is in the place of God, he is their mediator, their advocate, their priest. He will not minimise their part in the history, "ye thought evil against me" (v.20). That part can never be erased, nor be recovered, but God meant it unto good. God overturned and over-ruled to bring his own purpose to pass and to save many people alive.

Now we hear the language of comfort, "Fear ye not" (v.21). Fear is the opposite of faith, and he wants these men to be rid of fear. He says in fact, trust me, rely on me, I will nourish you. Every need shall be supplied for you and your little ones. The future generations shall know my bounty; "and he comforted them" (v.21), and spake kindly unto them. What an end to this life of sorrow, slander, misunderstanding, imprisonment and demotion! What lovely virtues are here manifested! He had shown prophetic features in his youth by his dreams. He had been invested with kingly dignity in the mature years of his life, now he shows priestly grace in the sunset of life. Youth should be marked by revelation, mature years by dignity, old age by sympathy.

When I first set out to note down these matters, I felt all the beauty of Joseph's life was when he was seventeen; then I thought when he was thirty how fittingly responsibility sat upon him; then the various incidents up to his age of fifty-six when he weeps over his father's face. But now to see Joseph at one hundred and ten years, can there be a beauty at such an age? (v.22). Here we see him with his children around him, but not just around him but the little ones, babes, upon his knees. The term implies not just a visit to great grandfather, but that he took an interest in their supervision. Woe betide the family who lose the influence of parents who have known God.

Hebrews 11:22 is the Spirit's commentary on his last moments. When he died he made mention of the departing of the children of Israel. Here at the end he is the prophet again. Prophetic truth engaged his mind, but then immediately he turns and does not mention but gives commandment. This is a matter of present moment, his bones. Prophetic matters are very important and nothing can invalidate them. God shall bring them to pass. But present truth must be adhered to. He gives commandment. John 14:1 shall come to pass: the Father's house, the many mansions, the marriage of the Lamb, the manifestation, and the eternal state. This is all secure in the purpose of God; but commandments have been given as to baptism, the Lord's Supper, to go into the world and preach the gospel, to love one another, and in symbol, carry the bones of Joseph. As centuries later the nation moved in the various wildernesses they would look at that coffin in which were Joseph's bones and say, "He preserved our life, he brought us to himself; he nourished us, stilled our fears and filled our hearts with promises of a good land and large, flowing with milk and honey." We also say this, and as we remember the Lord at the Lord's Supper, we recall His lonely life:

> *"Thy stainless life, Thy lovely walk*
> *In every aspect true,*
> *From the defilement all around*
> *No taint of evil drew.*
>
> *Morning by morning Thou did'st wake*
> *Amidst this poisoned air;*
> *Yet no contagion touched Thy soul,*
> *No sin disturbed Thy prayer."*

Joseph embalmed

God would have the memory of His servants embalmed or preserved. What God thinks of men of faith shall not be allowed to corrupt, and that which God has wrought in His servants He will cause the ages to remember. Over four hundred years will pass before that coffin will be laid to rest in the Cave of Machpelah, the parcel of ground Jacob gave to Joseph. Here he is laid to rest beside the great ones of God's reckoning, Abraham, Isaac and Jacob. We must stand back with wonder as the monument is raised to the greatest type of our Lord Jesus Christ ever recorded.

APPENDIX:

The Cedars of Lebanon

Note: This appendix is the verbatim transcript of a message our brother preached a short time before his Homecall. It is published as a reminder of his unique style and enthusiasm in the work of God.

Could we read again in the Psalms of David, 104 please. We'll commence to read at verse 10 of the hundred and fourth Psalm.

"He sendeth the springs unto the valleys, which run among the hills. They give drink to every beast of the field: the wild asses quench their thirst. By them shall the fowls of the heaven have their habitation, which sing among the branches. He watereth the hills from his chambers: the earth is satisfied with the fruit of thy works. He causeth the grass to grow for the cattle, and herb for the service of man: that he may bring forth food out of the earth; and wine that maketh glad the heart of man, and oil to make his face to shine, and bread which strengtheneth man's heart. The trees of the Lord are full of sap; the cedars of Lebanon, which he hath planted."

I would like to read that verse again. "The trees of the Lord are full of sap; the cedars of Lebanon, which he hath planted; Where the birds make their nests: as for the stork, the fir trees are her house. The high hills are a refuge for the wild goats; and the rocks for the conies. He appointed the moon for seasons: the sun knoweth his going down. Thou makest darkness, and it is night: wherein all the beasts of the forest do creep forth. The young lions roar after their prey, and seek their meat from God.

The sun ariseth, they gather themselves together and lay them down in their dens. Man goeth forth unto his work and to his labour until the evening. O Lord, how manifold are thy works! In wisdom hast thou made them all: the earth is full of thy riches."

May the Lord bless the public reading of His Word.

There are books in the Bible that are collated together, and I feel that this afternoon it would be God's intention that we stay in the book of the Psalms. I know it is generally a book where those who have become more mature, dwell in. But I have thought that there may be perhaps a message for every soul that's in the meeting, particularly in relation to the cedars of Lebanon.

The book of Job is basically a book of sorrows. It is the sad awful tale of how much a man suffered, as under the chastising hand of God, albeit, through the instrumentality of the devil. In the book of Job then, it is basically a book of sorrows. Very few lights ever shine in the book of Job, except those most remarkable statements that Job makes; those times when he is so severely crushed, he seems to let go those gems that we shall never forget even from the very first day we have read them; such as, when all has gone and children are gone and wealth is gone, and everything that man would set his heart upon is gone, and even though his wife would say to him, "Curse God and die, Job" – "though He slay me yet will I trust Him", and these jewels sparkle in the book of Job, and we could go on, but basically the book of Job is a book of sorrows.

But everyone that is young, they should be positively acquainted with the book of Proverbs. The book of Proverbs is simply and plainly a book of sayings. Why sayings? Of course, they came from what we would judge to be, and the Bible has confirmed, that there never was a man wiser than Solomon, before him or after him, and thus we must give at least an ear to the sayings of the wisest man that ever lived. That book is filled with sayings for the young and for the old, and for the mature and for the aged, and I feel that many of the problems that face my life, and many of the times I can't find an answer, is because of my great and gross ignorance of such a book as the book of the Proverbs.

Ecclesiastes comes under the category of these books that are grouped together, and I have always found the book of Ecclesiastes a very strange book. There are times when I feel that the man is most deeply spiritual, and there are times that I am convinced that there never was a man that was further away from God; and on the passing, when did you last read the book of the Ecclesiastes? You know, all God's Word is profitable, but in the book of the Ecclesiastes, if you read it when you go home and you get confused, remember that you are in the best of company for all of the greatest men who ever wrote anything on the book of Ecclesiastes were scratching their head to try and understand, in the same places that we have done. You see, Solomon wrote the Ecclesiastes sometimes when he was in good state with God, and other times when he wrote in it he was in bad state with God. So don't be too hard on Solomon because up every side here of the hall there are men and they're like the rest of us; often times they're in good state with God, and sometimes they feel they would like to write a book when they're in good state with God; but when we're in a bad state with God, my, we wouldn't want all our thoughts to be printed. But the Ecclesiastes has been printed, and that is why there are so many confusing things in that book.

The Song of Songs is of course a book of secrets. A book that very, very few people, even in the present day read, and of course, a book, if you don't read it, then there's no chance that you'll ever enjoy it.

But we're all clear this afternoon that the book of Psalms is basically a book of songs, a book of singing. Not all joy of course; every song is not hilarious. There are songs even in our ungodly state, they sobered us. There were others that gave us great sense of elation.

Then the book of the Psalms: there are times when you really feel delighted when you read the Psalms, and other times you feel cast down, in the depths of despair. I want to take no longer time to tell you some of my ramblings in the Psalms, but I want to say that this book of the Psalms has a very personal bearing upon us. Did you notice in this Psalm; I don't understand all the beginning of Psalm 104, I don't know very much about those chambers and about those winds and about all those mighty things of creation – you go home and read about them; but there are some things in the Psalm I do understand and the first thing that's impressed me in the Psalm is that God is cognisant about everything and God is cognisant of everybody. You see, who would ever take any interest whether the wild asses got a drink of water or not? Who in this hall has ever given a thought this week as to whether the grass is growing well that the cattle might get fed? Who is caring in this hall whether the young lion has had its food or not? Says someone, that has nothing to do with me, no, I know it has nothing to do with you, but I want to tell you that there's not a thing in life that is not recorded in Psalm 104, there's not a thing that God doesn't know. He knows where the lions hide out, He knows where the stork is, He knows the birds that sing in the branches of every tree and Psalm 104, let you and I take comfort in Psalm 104, God knows everything. You see, there are things that I would like to tell you about myself, but there are things that I would, with all my rigour, try to hide from you. But I want to tell you something, there is nothing in my life that God does not know about and there is nothing in your life that God does not know about.

I want to come down to the verse concerning the cedars of Lebanon. The cedars of Lebanon, they are full of sap. If God takes cognisance of the beasts, He takes cognisance of the birds, He takes cognisance of the very trees, the very trees, and He calls them the trees of the Lord. I want to show you some things about the cedar, then I want to apply it and show you some remarkable things I have taken time to discover, I think they're remarkable, but possibly I'm very, very easy pleased!

I want you to notice about these cedars, the first thing it says about them, that they are planted of the Lord. They are planted of the Lord. No human being ever planted the cedar trees. You may plant your daffodils, you may lay your roses out in the garden as best it suits you, but the cedars were all planted of the Lord, and not only were they planted of the Lord but they needed nothing from any other source to make them grow. The trees of the Lord are full of sap, and the cedar was planted of the Lord and it needed not man to touch it. It needed nothing to make it grow. It owed its complete existence, life and preservation to the Lord. I want that point to get over very forcibly because I want to make quite a bit of that. They were planted by the Lord and when the Lord planted these cedars they were planted in the most exposed position that ever anything could be planted in. They were planted in the top of the mountains of Lebanon. In fact, I have taken time to note that some of these trees, these cedars, were actually growing 6000 ft. above sea level. They grew to nearly, and possibly some more, over 100 ft. high. It has been known that their girth has been over 41 ft. and yet they have never been touched, they have never been watered, they have never ever known anything artificial from man, because they have been planted by the Lord. I pray that that simple point will get home.

The point I want to make out of that is this: that these trees have been planted in the most exposed position that they could ever have been in, and yet they grew. And yet they grew in height. And yet they grew in girth. And yet they flourished and blossomed and brought forth fruit. Oh, I pray that I'll not need to preach much after I've told you about that.

There are other things about them I must inform your mind. At the first glance at Lebanon, three things struck your eye. The Bible speaks about the stream that came out of Lebanon, the Bible speaks about the snow of Lebanon, then the Bible speaks about the cedars of Lebanon. Oh, the first thing that caught your eye about this cedar was its majesty and the next thing that caught your eye about it was that it was evergreen, that it was evergreen. Oh, I pray that God will give us a few minutes just to highlight these points.

The next point I want to show you about the cedar, it says the trees of the Lord are full of sap. You know that word sap doesn't need exegesis, does it now? You don't need me to give you a great long screed about what sap is. There's hardly an ordinary Christian who doesn't know when the ministry's sappy. What does this mean; it's full of sap? These great, mighty, majestic, evergreen cedars, they constantly, from their bark, emit resin. It never stopped coming out of it. The trees of the Lord are full of sap.

Let me now take time, by God's help, to point this out, that all those who are planted by God; all those who have been planted by God, all those who have the life of God within them, they need no substitute of earth for to make them grow. In this land in which we live, and in our christian experience, we are not here to harangue people what they go in for, we are not interested in that, but, we are here to tell you those who are planted of the Lord, they need no substitute to make them grow. Once a man and a woman have got salvation, the first evidence is that they desire the sincere milk of the word that they may grow thereby. Then they have greater desires for the strong meat of the word of God, and should every other man leave them, and should every other toy and trinket be taken away from them, they'll still stand. They need no substitute. They need no touching up from man for the trees of the Lord, the trees of the Lord are full of sap.

The last thing that we would like is to be put in an exposed position. The last thing that we would pray for is that we would have to face extreme and daily adversity; but, public and private lives, and history has recorded, that in all the ages of the church, that times of difficulty, poverty, privation and insecurity, where this world is concerned, have been the sweetest, deepest, dearest days in the Christian's experience. Aye brethren, is it not true that we love to shun adversity, and we love to shun exposed positions? But the cedar, it grew and it grew, and it grew and it became evident that it was growing. Not only up this way, but out this way and in every way. It mattered not dear Christian, how strong the winds upon mount Lebanon would blow, it would never uproot, it would never take out, it has never been known for a wind to take a cedar from Lebanon out of the ground. My friend, irrespective of how the winds of adversity may blow, even though you may feel the winds of poverty blowing, desertion by others, even your dear fellow Christians might not be too nice to you, remember this, if you are one of the trees of the Lord, it'll not matter how hard the wind may blow, it shall never take you, you're roots are down and they're deep and they're solid and you've been planted by the Lord.

Would you notice that, where the Lord caused them to grow, not only where it was most exposed, but he caused them to grow, I judge, in the region of 5000-6000 ft. above sea level. Notice the atmosphere in which these trees grow. They don't grow down in the well-watered plains of Sodom. They don't grow way down in the balmy south of Egypt. They don't grow among the cities. They grow away above earth level altogether. Why am I so barren? Why are there so few leaves in my life? Why is there so little blossom and fruit? It's because I live so long in the well-watered plains. For this tree to grow, the Lord planted it away above sea level, away above earth level, away up in the heights where it was near unto the God of heaven. My dear brethren, I don't know the most of you here, I hardly know anybody, but I know this much, as face answers to face in waters, so does the heart of man to man. We've tried everything to advance ourselves in the christian life. We thought when we were young if we had a good spiritual companion to go about the meetings with that that would help us. Then we thought if we got a good spiritual woman, that would help us. Then we thought if we could get into a good spiritual assembly, that would help us; and of course we've spent money and we've tried dozens of things to be more spiritual and all the time we don't want to accept that to grow in girth and height and in leaves and blossom and fruit, we must really get away beyond all the things and all the friends, and get to that place we heard about, and I must concur with this because it is true. It's only rare times that we know the secret of the Most High God. Let's get away up above it altogether. Colossian truth, isn't it? Set your affection on things above where Christ sitteth at the right hand of God. I'm a strong reader of Richard Baxter of Kidderminster and his 'Saint's Rest', and he said, "Why should I live in heaven?" Well, he said, "Don't think and don't feel awkward when the preacher says you should be living a heavenly life." I know by the faces of some people that they think some of the preachers are oddities. Brethren listen, Mr Richard Baxter said, "Why should my thoughts not be in heaven? My Saviour is there, my Lord is there, my Lover is there, my All is there." And how do you grow? It's by getting away up beyond, not only sea level, getting beyond city level, getting beyond people and things, and this old world, up into the heavenlies with Christ.

I would love to have spent more time on the majesty and beauty of this tree but I'm sure that you have at least caught that. The point that I want to stress at the moment is the vitality of the tree. The trees of the Lord are full of sap, full of sap. Brethren, I would like to ask us all, and I hope you don't fall asleep just at this juncture, for you know when the Lord preached they didn't sleep. It says all the eyes of them in the synagogue were fastened upon Him. Vitality! Vitality! There was from this tree a momentary resin that could be seen, that could be touched, that could be known. I believe every man and woman that has the grace of God and the indwelling Spirit, it is God's divine intention that they should be marked by spiritual vitality, spiritual vitality. There should be exuding from the people of God the very life of God Himself. Says someone, that is very high – but it really isn't. Surely when we got God's salvation we not only had an experience but we got the Son of God. "He that hath the Son of God hath life." Mary conceived the Son of God and it could not be hid. Surely when you and I were saved that's what more or less happened to us. Christ began to form within you and I: "Christ in you the hope of glory", "that Christ may be formed in you".

My dear fellow Christian, I feel that like the trees of the Lord that are planted upon mount Lebanon, they are full, full, they are full of sap.

There are things now I want you to notice before we finish. The leaves, the leaves on the cedar, they never ever, they never ever wither. The leaves on the cedar, they never, ever, wither. First of all I want to point out to you that the leaves speak of an evidence of divine life. At home we have so many large trees and you would think that you would like to cut the half of them down, but when you wait to the spring again there you see the little shoots coming up and they begin to take form and out come leaves. You see, as long as there's leaves it is the evidence of life. I'm a thorough believer that everyone who names the name of Christ, there should be a positive evidence of divine life, a positive evidence of divine life.

The next thing that was most remarkable about the cedar was the blossom on the cedar. Those who have travelled in these lands, I have not, possibly I'm sorry about that, but they say that the blossom of the cedar is one of the most magnificent sights to be seen. I remember being in London once, I've been there a few times, but this once anyway, I was in Kent at the time when the apple and the cherry blossoms were out. I've never seen a sight in our land like it. The beauty of the blossom, but you know when you see the blossom on your apple or on your cherry tree, the blossom speaks of promise; promise of something that is yet to come. I wonder if there is promise in us. I wonder if the elders looked over the assembly this morning and saw in it young men of promise. I wonder when you look into the faces of the little children that you sit normally with in the Sunday School, I wonder if there's promise.

On that point, I'll take a minute to encourage those who work in the Sunday School. I think it's a most noble work. I was engaged in it for a long, long time and thus I'm clear to speak about it. In a German school one day, the inspector came round. You all remember when the inspectors came round the school, I'm very sure you do anyway, and when the inspector came round, he went round every class; and this morning he called on this man and he was the headmaster with his class and there he was and he sat there before the master came in, and when the children came in they all sat in their seat and the master saluted the children. Well, when we were at school, we all stood up and we normally saluted the headmaster or the lady that was teaching and in all the schools of Germany, every child saluted the teacher except in one class. The inspector thought that it was time that this might be righted, that there might be honour for the teacher and for the older generation and I understand all that, but when he asked the master, "Why do the children sit and you salute them?" He says, "Well, it is like this, sir, you would never know who is in your class." "You would never know who is in your class" - what he meant - you would never know what future man might be in your class and from that class came the man that Mr Wilson mentioned, and I suggest that all the brethren should read his life story again, that beloved man called Martin Luther. "You never know who is in your class!" You don't know who will go and take the gospel further than you have ever been able to do and while the laws of convention would have it otherwise let us see to it that we remember the blossom.

I hope you live in hope in your meeting. I've never been here before. I hope you live in hope, I do pray you do. Live in hope that the young men will be holy. Live in hope that the young women will be godly. Live in hope and pray that they might be better men than ever you and I have ever been. That's the prayer of spiritual men, to pray that the people that are coming on will be a hundred times better than ever we have been. I would judge it would take them to be that in the days that are coming upon us. Full of blossom, that's promise!

The cedars of Lebanon were always loaded down with fruit. Full of produce! I think it's only twice in the recent five years of preaching at conferences and meetings, that I've heard anyone speaking about bearing fruit, bearing fruit. My dear brethren, I pray that we are exercised about bearing fruit. Bearing fruit unto God, bearing fruit amongst our fellow Christians and bearing fruit in the salvation of poor men and women. My dear brethren, I know nothing about Fort William, I know nothing about many of the Irish meetings, but I can tell you there's not much fruit nowadays. The saddest thing is there's very few people exercised about bringing forth fruit unto God. There may be blossom, but blossom's no use without fruit. Oh, pray God earnestly, that there might be much fruit seen amongst us. It is said by the travellers who travel, that when they got to mount Lebanon, the only thing that crossed their mind was to get under the shade of the cedar tree. Oh, the mighty shade of the wonderful cedar tree. Dear brethren, I've seen a peace and tranquillity under the cedar tree. Is it too naïve to say, I wonder when last we were a shade to other people? I wonder when you last did someone a kindly deed. I wonder when you last took the burning heat out of someone's weary journey. Are you a refuge in your assembly? Are you a comfort to all that come in contact with you? Or are you a difficult type of person, are you a person who's hard to approach and no one would come near you? This tree was full of shade, full of shade. I wonder if people are happy in your company, or are you very difficult to get on with? You know, even some preachers are difficult to get on with. I don't give much for any of them and I don't give anything for any Christian that's very difficult to get on with. Spiritual men and women should be easy to be entreated, easy to be approached, kind and gentle and true. Full of shade, full of shade. I want to ask the entire meeting again, I know in your meeting there are people that could do with a little shade. Says someone, but you've not been to our meeting – but I've been among human beings for quite a long time! In our meeting there's a lot of people who could do with a little shade, a little comfort. That's part of the ministry you know. Anyone that ministers and doesn't minister comfort, they've missed the mark. It is to edification, but remember, it is to comfort. The shade of the great tree!

I enjoyed this in my soul when I noticed that the singing birds were in the branches. The singing birds were in the branches. I don't know if you noticed the birds today. Do you know that they thank God before you got up out of your bed this morning? The birds were giving God thanks before they even had a bite to eat. I love that about the beautiful lark. It's just beginning to come into our country. As it was up in the morning without one little bit in its stomach, it gets up into the sky and it praises its God, praises its God. Singing birds in the branches!

The cedar was full of praise, full of praise. Not only peace and produce and promise, but it was full of praise. Are you a happy Christian? Are you? I never was happy until I got salvation. Full of praise! Are you one of the singing birds? The Bible says about every Christian, he's to be marked by singing and making melody in his heart unto the Lord, unto the Lord. You may disagree with me, you may, but I'll not be huffed at you. I have discovered that in my daily life, even singing praises to God, I have discovered it to be an act of worship. Have you ever noticed a singing person? They're generally happy. Oh, I'm not talking about flighty people and I don't want to give you the impression that I am singing choruses all the days of my life, but what I do want to get over to you is this, that because of the wonders of God's grace and the person of the Lord Jesus and the wonders of the heaven we are yet to go to, we should be a most happy and praiseful people before the Lord. There were singing birds in the branches.

Not only so, but there was always round about the cedar tree and after the fruit had fallen, there was always the evidence of seed. What was that to tell us? That was to tell us there was going to be propagation, there was going to be more cedar trees as time went on.

My time is short! What was this cedar made for? There came a time when the axe came upon it, and then there came a time when the plane came upon it. Then there came a time when the square was put upon it and this tree was taken down, and it was cut and it was planed and it was squared and it was used, that it might adorn and decorate the holy sanctuary of God.

One day you and I are going to adorn the courts of glory, but in the meantime there's the cutting down, there's the planing and there's the squaring before we'll ever adorn the house of God. I know that has a setting locally and that could be well applied, but I want to tell you something: the Lord is changing us all just now, but what we'll be like in the coming day, what the cedar was in the mountain and what it was in the house of the Lord was two distinct things altogether. Oh, may there be a resin come out of us, evidence of spiritual vitality, for the trees of the Lord are full of sap - the cedars of Lebanon.

Shall we pray.

Our God and our Father, we bow in Thy holy presence and bless Thee for these hours we've spent before Thee. We thank Thee for reading to us that delightful Psalm that tells us of that home that we dearly long for, Thy holy presence. We confess before Thee we are not what we would like to be and we feel we're not even what people think we are, but Lord, Thou dost know that we long after Thee with the deepest longings of our breast and we pray of Thee, Thou wilt teach us in Thy ways. Thou wilt break us up and Thou indeed would conform us to Thy Son. Make, O God and Father, to have positive objectives in our lives. Grant, O God, that we might see in our lives, e'er we die, something of not only promise but something of produce, some fruit for Thee. Thus we'd remember every class of person in the meeting. We thank Thee for all those that are Thine. Would'st Thou save any that are not saved and give them that divine life. Remember the other meetings and would'st Thou remember Lord, our dear brother who is lying ill in Dublin. We plead with Thee, Thou indeed would remember him too. Thus we commend ourselves to Thee and pray Thy blessing in parting, in His Holy Name – Amen.